Banshees, Beasts and Brides from the Sea

Irish Tales of the Supernatural

Bob Curran

Appletree Press

*For my wife, Mary, without whose
patience and encouragement this book
would never have been written*

First published by
The Appletree Press Ltd
19–21 Alfred Street
Belfast BT2 8DL
1996

A catalogue record for this book is available
from the British Library

ISBN 0 86281 553 3

9 8 7 6 5 4 3 2 1

Contents

Introduction

My fascination with folktales, particularly those connected with the supernatural, came in differing ways from my maternal grandparents by whom I was raised. My grandfather, who came from south Armagh, was a widely known, well-respected musician who had a fund of old stories with which he continually regaled visitors to our house. My grandmother, on the other hand, was a hard-headed Ballymena woman who, whilst dismissing as "nonsense" many of the old tales, still allowed her home to be used as a "ceili-house", a gathering place for all those who came to see my grandfather.

I grew up in a country area, on the edge of the Mourne Mountains in County Down, where my grandmother kept a small post-office and shop. She opened at six o'clock in the morning to catch the passing trade to Belfast and closed at six o'clock at night. The only problem was that the evening paper – the *Belfast Telegraph* – was delivered from a bus at a quarter to seven. This meant that anyone who wanted their *Telegraph* that evening had to come to our back door and often came on into the house to see my grandfather. My grandmother, tolerant woman that she was, put up with the human traffic which gathered in our kitchen late into the night – the musicians from deeper into the mountains, the poteen-makers from the bogs along the road and the neighbours who had dropped in for a chat and who often stayed longer than any of us had intended.

Around the black range in my granny's kitchen, the country people gathered to warm themselves, to smoke a pipe or to "tell a yarn or two". We had no electricity and the room was lit by gas-lamps, suspended from the ceiling, and the ruddy glow which the grate threw out. In such a setting, the talk usually began with general gossip of the countryside and soon turned to tales of ghosts and fairies. One story often led to another and slowly the surrounding countryside, which had seemed so friendly in daylight, became a world of fear where goblins and banshees lurked around every turn of the night-bound roads.

Sitting in a corner by the side of the range, I allowed these frightening stories to swirl around me. And late at night I would lie awake in bed listening to the call of owls in the rath (fairy fort) behind the house, or to the wheels of a cart going past on the road. I would imagine these sounds to be either the souls of the dead, crying for their release from purgatory, or a fearful fairy coach which carried those ghosts which had recently passed over to the after-life.

My grandfather was also very friendly with a number of individuals whom he called "tramp clergymen". These were walking men from all over the country, many of them musicians in their own right. They would often call to play a tune or two with us, to cadge a meal from my grandmother or to swap stories. "They are worse than the regular clergy", my grandfather would say, "for they'll sit and preach at you all day if you'll let them." And indeed this was so, for once such men got their feet below the table they told stories about their travels for as long as they had a listener.

These experiences gave me an ear for such tales which has never left me. Later, as I began to travel around the countryside myself, I began to pick up the local tales in the areas I visited.

A good storyteller needs three things in my view – a good memory (so that the tale is remembered), a good imagination (so that the tale can be embellished if need be) and good oral skills (so that the tale can be told). Many of the people I have come across, although having little formal education, have possessed these attributes and the stories which they told me have stuck in my memory across the years.

The stories, however, had another function. They provided a way of interpreting and of looking at the world which often came from a time long past. Nowadays it is, of course, easy to ascribe such tales to the superstitiousness and gullibility of our forebears but the lore serves to establish a psychological context in which events were explained and described which is as much a part of social history as formal texts or recorded data. Folklore, therefore, needs to be preserved as an important window into the past.

Sadly, the art of story-telling in country areas, once carried out by skilled practitioners, is becoming largely a thing of the past. In an era where most of our interpretations and knowledge of the world come from a box in the corner of the sitting-room or from the daily newspapers, and at a time when oral skills are in a steady decline, many of these old tales are disappearing into obscurity. Happily, however, there is now some attempt amongst local history groups to capture some of them before they vanish completely but I suspect that this may actually be the last generation to be able to record such material.

As my own contribution to the process of maintaining these traditional country tales and as a belated tribute to the people who told them, I have set down a number in this book. These are mostly tales which I have collected across the Irish countryside – each one dealing with the supernatural in some shape or form. They are the voices of the country people and I hope as you read them, you can hear the wind soughing in the trees beyond the window-pane, or catch the waft of the sweet-scented smoke curling up from the peat fire in the open hearth. If you do, then it will all have been worthwhile.

Bob Curran
Portrush 1996

The Mark of the Beast

According to an old book entitled The Travels of Cosmo (1669), *Ireland was once known to the English as "Wolfland" on account of the number of those wild animals which were to be found there. Wolves were a particular menace right across the country. Diaries and letters from travellers throughout the land speak of great packs of wild wolves roaming freely and attacking lone cottages and even the outskirts of towns during the winter months when food was scarce. During a particularly severe winter in 1661 the outskirts of Belfast were ravaged by packs of the starving animals and those journeying to the town of Lisburn, several miles distant, did so in mortal fear of their lives. It was instances such as these which caused Sir John Ponsonby to introduce a Parliamentary Bill of Grievances in 1662 "to encourage the killing of wolves and foxes in Ireland". Ten years earlier Oliver Cromwell had issued a stern edict at Kilkenny forbidding the export of Irish Wolfhounds (a dog specially bred to destroy the animals), so serious had the problem of wolves become. Indeed, the years 1640 to 1650 were some of the worst experienced – the upheavals and slaughter of the Irish Rebellion had led to an increased number of unburied corpses and a concomitant increase in the Irish wolf population. Those dwelling along the edges of the Wicklow Mountains, the Sperrins, or in Monaghan and Kildare felt themselves especially at risk as packs living in those areas roamed the countryside.*

By the late-eighteenth century, however, the number of wolves was in rapid decline in almost every part of Ireland. Advances in weaponry (with the development and widespread use of the musket) and the clearing of forests which were the animals' natural habitat, had reduced their number. By 1810, apart from a few isolated groups reputedly still to be found in the Wicklow Hills, wolves had all but disappeared from the Irish countryside. Tradition has it that the last wolf in Ireland was actually killed in the Sperrin Mountains of Tyrone by a wolf-hunter named Rory Carragh around the late 1790s but there may well have been single animals still living in remote areas after that.

The following story gives a flavour of the dangers of travelling through wolf-infested country.

The Fiddler and the Wolves

"A fiddler was passing one day through the woods of Wicklow near to some mountain country which was reputedly infested by wolves. He had a knapsack on his back, filled with bread and cheese which he had procured by playing in a town nearby.

He had been travelling for a long time and was extremely tired, so he sat down in the shade of a great tree, opened the knapsack and prepared to eat. Imagine his horror when, looking up, he saw a number of large grey wolves prowling at a distance from him and eyeing him hungrily. They circled so close that the fiddler became in fear of his life and tossed them a couple of scraps from the knapsack which they quickly devoured. Then they began to circle him again, drawing ever closer and still fixing him with long and hungry stares. Terrified, the fiddler dug even deeper into his knapsack and threw a few more crusts of bread and a rind of cheese in their direction. The wolves snapped these up and once more began to circle the tree, their tongues lolling out of the corners of their mouths and saliva dripping from their jaws. The fiddler was now certain that he was going to provide a meal for the creatures but still he was determined to see if he could in some way save himself. So he dug into the knapsack once again and this time drew out a large loaf of bread and a hunk of cheese which he tossed in the direction of the advancing animals. The wolves ate these up quickly and, the moment they had finished, eyed the fiddler once more.

A cold sweat was now breaking on the poor man's brow and he wondered if he could even yet in some way save himself from becoming a feast for the wild wolves. He had one last card to play: deep in the bottom of his knapsack was a roasting fowl which he had been saving for later. But what was a meal to him if he were to be eaten by animals? With a sigh, he pulled it out and tossed it to the wolves, intent on making his escape whilst they fought over it. The animals, however, consumed the bird in an instant and turned back to circle the fiddler once more.

There now seemed no hope and the fiddler concluded that he was doomed. Wearily, he snatched up his fiddle, intent on playing a final air before the wolves got him. No sooner had he drawn the bow across the strings and played the first notes, however, than the advancing wolves stopped. He began to play a little more and the creatures turned tail and fled back towards the mountains.

There is an old superstition which is common in Wicklow, and in many other parts of Ireland besides, that wolves have no souls and mortal music reminds them of that. Anyway, these creatures took to their heels and were soon gone.

In anger the fiddler shook his fist and called after them, all the while eyeing his now empty knapsack which had formerly contained his meal:

'A pox upon you all! Had I known that you were so fond of my music, I would have gladly played to you *before* dinner!' "

The above story is most probably based on a seventeenth-century joke or "pleasant tale" related by a Sir Thomas Fairfax and formally recorded in 1624. The notion that no animal could listen to human music was widespread throughout many parts of Ireland and it was commonly supposed that to drive away foxes from hen-runs one had only to play a series of notes on a tin whistle.

Ireland was, of course, and continues to be a great hunting country. One of the most famous stories about wolves that we have from the Irish comes in the form of an old poem, "McDermot", supposedly composed in the early 1700s and dealing with the procession of a wolf-hunt through Munster.

During the seventeenth and early-eighteenth centuries, the number of wolves prowling the Irish countryside increased dramatically for a time. This led to a new trade amongst a small number of Irishmen, that of wolf-hunter. Farmers whose flocks and herds were being ravaged by the animals, especially during the winter months, were willing to pay skilled hunters to put an end to the pestilence in their area. Thus, a few men made a precarious living at hunting down the beasts, setting traps and snares and sometimes actually facing the wolves in their lairs with loaded muskets. Those who did so were brave individuals and were also few and far between. Most Irish wolf-hunters simply resorted to poisoned bait and spring traps to catch their quarry.

However, despite the traps which were set for them, some wolves continually managed to avoid the machinations of the wolf-hunters, displaying an almost human cunning and wariness. This gave rise to old tales that some of the creatures were not true wolves at all but rather human beings who had, for one reason or another, been turned into animal form. Some were even believed to be local wizards who had taken on wolf-form in order to create mischief among their neighbours.

The most famous of all Irish wolf-hunters, according to folklore, is Rory Carragh. Although little is known about Carragh himself, he is credited with magical skills which aided him in his work and brought about the end of his most famous quarry, the wolf known as Old Greycoat. This version of the story comes from the lands of Counties Monaghan and Tyrone on the edge of the Sperrins.

Rory Carragh and Old Greycoat

"Those were bad times in Tyrone without a doubt. It was around the spring of 1780, I heard, and the winter which had gone before had been particularly severe. There were still wolves in Ireland in those days and the weather had been just as sore on them as it had been on the humans. Most of them had died out, killed by cold and hunger, but there was still one or two of them, high up in the Sperrin Mountains. As soon as lambing came round, they descended in ragged packs and had to be driven off with fire and muskets. The hunger had made them so desperate and incautious that many were killed before they could get anywhere near the sheepfolds to snatch away lambs.

There was one wolf, however, that had avoided the best efforts of the farmers and local hunters and continued to carry away newborn lambs and small children as well, I've heard it said. This creature seemed to have an almost human intelligence and was able to outwit all the men that were sent against him and avoid all the traps that were laid for him. He was known in the locality as 'Old Greycoat' since he had a long, grey pelt and seemed to be one of the oldest and wiliest wolves in the district. No one knew where his lair might be and he always struck at edge of twilight so that nobody could see where he went or follow him.

At last his ravages and plunderings got so bad that the farmers and shepherds along the Tyrone border decided that something serious had to be done about him. Now at this time there were wolf-hunters in Ireland – men who made a living out of hunting down wolves and killing them for the local people – and the Tyrone shepherds had heard of a man who worked away down in the South of Ireland named Rory Carragh. They said that he was one of the best wolf-hunters in the whole of the country. This was because he was part wolf himself. There was an old story about him that he had been abandoned by his mother and had been raised by a she-wolf somewhere around the Maamturk Mountains in Galway, so he knew wolves and their ways and was well able to trap them. It was said that he never failed and it was Rory Carragh that the shepherds of Tyrone sent for.

At that time, Carragh was away hunting wolves deep in the Wicklow Mountains and it was several weeks before he came to Tyrone. He arrived one frosty morning, riding on a dark horse, through a slight flurry of rain which had sprung up just before his arrival. He was a tall, rangy, old-looking man – slightly stooped – with a long, dark face and thick iron-grey hair tucked under the brim of a soft, wide hat. He wore sober, dark clothes, badly stained with the dirt and travel of his long journey from Wicklow, and across his shoulders he had slung a long-barrelled hunting rifle which looked a fearsome weapon indeed. Rattling loudly against the flanks of his horse were a number of spring traps which the hunter used to catch his adversaries. Behind him, on a small pony, rode a young boy of about twelve or thirteen years, thin and feral-looking, with the same sort of ranginess which characterised the wolf-hunter; he gave those whom he passed a long brooding stare which seemed out of place for one so young. The farmers assumed this to be Carragh's son but were afraid to ask the strange, silent man. They made the two of them welcome in a little roadside inn on the very edge of the Sperrins. The wolf-hunter dismounted and made his way into the building with a long, loping stride which reminded the farmers of the gait of a wild animal.

'I am come', says Carragh in a low, husky voice that suggested the bark of a wolf to some of those present, 'because I am told that you have a particular problem in this country.'

One of the farmers stepped forward and told him about Old Greycoat and of the devastation which the wolf was causing in the district. The wolf-hunter listened carefully, sitting forward from time to time as though deeply interested, his yellow, dog-like eyes narrowing slightly, whilst the boy sat in the corner of the inn, never saying a word but watching Carragh with a fearful intensity as a cub might watch its wolf-father. Indeed, some of the farmers later admitted as to not being certain whom they feared more – Old Greycoat itself or the evil-looking wolf-hunter whom they had brought amongst them.

When they had finished, Carragh nodded slowly.

'This wolf is surely a terrible one', he said in his thick voice, 'and may require special measures.' Then he named his price, which was high, but the shepherds could just about pay it and they deemed it money well spent if it finished Old Greycoat. They agreed to pay what the wolf-hunter asked.

'Now we will eat', said Rory Carragh, motioning to the boy.

'When the light begins to fail, I will consider my business here.'

Food was brought and he and the boy ate it, quickly and ravenously and with their hands, like wild beasts. Then they slept for a time until the sun was beginning to set. The shepherds of Tyrone watched them and wondered what manner of mortals they were for they seemed to have the ways of the wolves about them.

As the sun was starting to go down, Rory Carragh stirred and shook the boy who rose sleepily. He called the shepherds to him.

'Now', says he, 'show me where you pen your sheep and we'll try to work out what Old Greycoat will get up to when he comes sneaking down to attack your flocks.'

At this time, the shepherds folded their sheep for safety in a pen which was enclosed by high stone walls, with gaps for entrance and exit at each end. These gaps were secured with stout wooden gates but, despite the strength of these obstacles, the wolves were still able to break in and ravage the sheltering flocks. Rory Carragh surveyed the stone sheep-pen thoughtfully. His line of sight followed up the hill where an old gully ran down from the mountain and along the side of the pen.

'If the wolf is as crafty as you say he is', says he, pointing with a time-worn finger, 'that's the way he might come down from his mountain hideout.' The shepherds followed his finger and were forced to agree with him but they were also quick to point out that Old Greycoat might also attack from the other side of the pen. Rory considered and nodded slowly.

'Then', says he, addressing the boy, 'you will guard one side of the pen tonight and I will guard the other side next the gully. This Greycoat attacks with the stealth of a cat so be upon your guard until morning. If he does attack, then rivet him with a spear through the neck but make sure that it is firmly embedded into him or else he will rise up and tear you apart. If, however, he attacks from the other side, from the gully, then I will call to you and you must come immediately for this one is a wily character indeed.'

He then asked around to see if any of the shepherds and farmers from the area would stay with the boy to keep an eye on him and give them a hand in capturing the wolf, but the cowardly men were content to go to their beds and leave a boy guarding part of their sheepfold. A boy was expendable, they argued, whereas trained shepherds were not and they needed to give further thought to the matter from the safety of their own homes. Rory Carragh merely shrugged at such cowardice and motioned the boy to his post at the side of the sheepfold. He went, taking a heavy pike with him with which to spear the wolf.

Night fell across the mountains and Rory Carragh and the boy waited in the darkness. All was silent. Then, from far away, came the single, high-pitched howl of a wolf. The boy shivered and clutched his pike more tightly, while on the other side of the sheepfold Rory Carragh's eyes narrowed and he seemed to sniff at the air like a dog. The wolf howled once more and was silent for a time. Then the sound came again, slightly closer this time. It was answered by the bark of a dog on a neighbouring farm, but apart from that there was no other sound in the darkness. The pair of them waited in the gloom but there was no further sound. The night was dark and completely still.

Old Greycoat attacked from the side of the pen next the gully. He came slipping down, staying on the edge of the depression, moving stealthily between patches of shadow, keeping low on his belly as he went. Then he darted into the shadow of the wall and waited. Rory Carragh was almost dozing against the barrel of his long rifle when he chanced to hear a faint sound and started up.

At first he saw nothing under the moonlight but then his practised eye made out a thick, dark shadow which moved amongst the others. Taking a few steps forward, he approached it, raising the wolf-gun as he did so. For an instant the shadow stood stock still and the wolf-hunter thought that he had been mistaken. Then Greycoat struck, leaping forward in a mighty bound with teeth bared and ready for the fight. Another man would have been overcome by the suddenness and ferocity of the attack and would have been hurled to the ground, but not Rory Carragh. He twisted out of the way of the leaping animal so that Greycoat's fangs only caught him a glancing blow as the body of the creature hurtled past him. The wolf thudded against the wall of the sheep-pen but in a second it had turned, regained its feet, and was coming at him again. Rory raised the musket as a defence against a second leap. There was no time for him to prime the weapon and, as Greycoat came forward once more, he lashed out with the barrel, sending the wolf spinning to one side and calling out to the boy as he did so. The child came running with his pike in hand.

'There!' cried Rory Carragh. 'Pike him now!' And the boy raised the ancient pike and swiped at the snarling beast. His aim was bad, however, and the sharp end of the pike grazed the wolf just above the foreleg. It was not a mortal wound but it gave Rory Carragh enough time to draw a stabbing-sword from his belt and strike out at the wolf with it. The animal howled and fell back but the hunter was relentless, rushing forward and cutting and thrusting with the short-sword, following the beast as it retreated. By this time the boy had gathered up the musket and was fixing it, ready for firing.

Old Greycoat, seeing that the game was up for that night, turned and, before either Rory or the boy could properly aim the musket at him, vanished into the gloom of the mountain night. In the morning it was found that he had left a trail of blood from the pike-wound right across the bare rock and away toward his lair, high among the Sperrin peaks.

'We can track him now', Rory Carragh told the shepherds who gathered at first light to see and hear what had transpired, 'for yon' trail will lead us directly to him. But he'll be even more dangerous now – a wounded animal is always more desperate than a cunning one. Now, which one of you will come with me?' And he turned his smokey gaze towards the farmers and shepherds round about. They, true to their former cowardice, turned away and told the wolf-hunter that he could track down the beast himself as best he could. Rory Carragh nodded to the boy, who drew close to him, and together the pair of them set off for the wild slopes of the Sperrins.

The trail of gore led through ditches, across rocky fields and over stone dykes, higher and higher along the twisting trails. They passed through deep gullys and gloomy glens until they were deep in the heart of the mountain country. At last they came to a remote glen which seemed to be deeper and gloomier than all the others. Perched on the edge of it were the ruins of an ancient chapel and it was to these tumbled stones that the trail of blood eventually led. Rory and the boy circled the fallen walls and peered into the various openings along their length. The wolf-hunter looked down into an ancient crypt and there he saw a wolf-bitch lying with a litter of small, newly born pups. This was Greycoat's mate and she appeared to be just as vicious as he for she started up and made for the man as he stood in the opening. Rory Carragh, however, was ready for her and blasted her with a shot of his long-barrelled rifle. The she-wolf fell away, back into the darkness of the crypt, and the wolf-hunter quickly knelt down to fix his weapon once more. And he was not a moment too soon, for a wounded Greycoat leapt out from behind a great tombstone and made to attack again. The boy gave a cry of warning and Rory Carragh looked up in time to see the wolf coming straight for him. He managed to discharge a shot which caught the leaping creature full in the belly and threw it over on itself.

It was the end of Greycoat for the beast rolled over and did not rise again. Walking forward, Rory Carragh and the boy stood over its fallen form and, as they did so, the wolf-shape began to shimmer and melt in front of their eyes. They found themselves looking down on the thin body of an old man with a withered and cruel-looking face. Turning back to the ruined church, Carragh found that the wolf-bitch had turned into an old, thin-looking woman who lay curled up in a ball, like a wolf asleep. Greycoat and his mate had been werewolves, but in death they had reverted to their original shapes.

'It is as I thought', said Rory Carragh, crossing himself for protection. 'Some black evil has been wrought in this lonely place long ago and turned these ancient people into the forms of Greycoat and his mate. Now there is work to be done here for this site of evil must be purified.'

And so saying, he and the boy gathered brushwood and fallen branches and piled them within the ruined walls, then set them alight. The bodies of Greycoat and his mate, together with the still-mewling wolf-cubs, were completely burned as the flames rose higher into the thin mountain air. Smoke billowed in great clouds from the burning place across the gloomy valley below as Rory Carragh and the boy turned away towards the lowlands again.

The farmers of Tyrone paid the wolf-hunter what they owed

him and without a further word or a single backward glance Rory Carragh mounted his horse and rode off south, with the boy following him on his pony.

Old Greycoat was supposed to be the last wolf killed in Ireland but I'm not so sure about that for I did hear that Rory Carragh was killed sometime afterwards by wolves in the Kerry Mountains. But the boy lived on and became a great man in Ireland and a renowned hunter and trapper in his own right. At least that's what I was told."

The above story may or may not be true. Certainly, the character of Rory Carragh himself changes with the tales that are told about him. In one version of the above story he is described as a young man, "golden-haired and with a pleasant, sun-freckled face". In others he is a "gloomy, dark man, grim-looking and without a hint of a smile about his mouth", whilst in others still he appears as "a young man and a shepherd of Tyrone". No mention is made in most of the stories of a boy who travels with him, although in one tale his helper is a young Tyrone boy from one of the villages round about. In almost every tale he catches Greycoat in a wolf-trap, the above variation being the exception to this rule. One theme runs through every story, however, that of the wolves turning into human form as they die. They are, in fact, werewolves.

The motif of the werewolf is strong in Irish folklore. There are a number of old tales about strange tribes of wolf-men living in remote areas of County Tipperary, whose assistance was often sought by the ancient kings of Ireland when they made war upon each other. There are also tales of strange beings – half-men, half-wolves – roaming the remote forest and mountain areas of the island. Indeed, one of the oldest written stories that we have about werewolves comes from Ireland. This comes from the pen of Giraldus Cambrensis who wrote down many old Irish tales. The events are supposed to have taken place just a few years before his arrival in Ireland in 1185.

The Werewolves of Ossory

"Several years before the arrival of Prince John in Ireland, a certain priest was travelling from the kingdom of Ulster towards Meath on some urgent and religious business. With him travelled a young boy, a novice at one of the religious houses in Ulster, as a kind of squire or helpmate on his travels. Their journey was a long and arduous one which took them through much strange and brooding country where the people still kept close to the old pagan ways.

One evening, as the sun was setting, they reached a great and sprawling wood which ran along the borders of Meath and was known far and wide as part of the ecclesiastical See of Ossory. Dark was coming quickly, and the priest decided that the edge of the forest might make a good place to camp for the night. Accordingly, he lit a small fire, both for warmth and to keep wild forest animals away, and he and the boy prepared a simple evening meal for themselves.

As night drew on, the violet sky overhead changed to a deeper hue and soon utter darkness spread across the entire countryside. The small fire burned low and the boy lay half-dozing whilst the holy man pored over his religious books. Whilst he was so doing, he suddenly became aware that the sounds from the neighbouring woodlands, which had been quite loud at a time, had fallen away and an eerie silence pervaded the area. It was a strange thing and it badly frightened the priest for he was on holy business and was well aware that the Evil One was abroad on the road and was seeking to divert his path. Then, from the darkness beyond the fireglow came a voice, soft and gruff, but with a hint of urgency about it.

'Father!' it said. The priest looked towards the boy who appeared to be lying fast asleep. Thinking that he had imagined it, he turned back to the pages of his book. But the voice came again, harsh and insistent: 'Father!'

Rising, the priest closed his sacred book and walked to the edge of the fireglow. Standing there, he looked out into the darkness of the forest beyond.

'Who's there?' he asked, grasping the crucifix which hung about his neck, for he was sorely afraid of the machinations of the Evil One. 'Who calls me?'

For a moment there was silence, then the same harsh voice came again.

'A penitent sinner who seeks only your blessing, Father', it replied.

The priest clutched the crucifix even more tightly for he knew that Satan was the father of all lies, and that this might be a wily ruse to lure him into the darkness of the forest where he might be set upon by demons. Nevertheless, he took another step forward.

'If you are truly a repentent sinner', he said sternly, 'step forward into the firelight and reveal yourself so that I may hear your sins and grant you absolution.'

There was a long pause and the darkness in front of the holy man appeared to deepen slightly. The voice came again.

'I – I cannot, Father. I am under a severe curse and if you were to see me, you would find my appearance strange.'

It spoke with such pathos that the priest found himself quite moved. He peered against the darkness but could see nothing, save the movement of bushes in a light evening wind. When he spoke again, his tone was less stern and commanding.

'In my travels all across this country', he said kindly, 'I have seen many awful deformities. I have seen lepers and those who were born with terribly twisted bodies and faces. I have looked into countenances which were almost too terrible to gaze upon and I have given succour to those who were most sorely afflicted. I have seen men living under the most terrible of curses. So I doubt if anything that you can show me will alarm or disgust me. I therefore ask you again to come forward and let me gaze upon you so that I can see to whom it is that I grant the Lord's absolution.'

He waited but there was no response from the night for a long, long while. Then the voice came again, still harsh, yet breaking with emotion.

'If you were to see me', it told the priest, 'you would be greatly afraid. And, in truth, it is not absolution for myself which brings me so close to your fire but rather it is to seek absolution for she who cannot come.'

The priest was puzzled but he answered earnestly and in the same kindly tone.

'Tell me, are you diseased in some way?' he asked.

'After a fashion', answered the voice. 'But, Father, my form is so terrifying that you would be struck with fear if you were to behold it.'

The priest answered, using the same kindly tone.

'I have God's word and His goodness and power to protect me', he said. 'Why should I be frightened by one of His creatures? Please, I beg you as a priest, come into the light so that I may see you and give you the blessing for which you ask.'

By this time the boy had wakened and was now sitting by the edge of the fire looking out into the darkness with eyes that were wide and full of terror. He was only a novice and was unsettled by the strange, bodiless, growling voice. The priest motioned him to sit still and be quiet.

'Come forward!' he repeated. 'You cannot frighten me!'

There was a movement in the darkness beyond the firelight and into the wan circle of brilliance came a huge grey wolf, its muzzle white and dripping and its tongue lolling out of the side of its mouth. The priest crossed himself in shock and the boy made to cry out but was struck dumb by terror.

'There!' said the wolf in that familiar voice. 'Now you see me! Are you not terrified?' The priest was fairly choking with fear but yet he shook his head.

'I – I am protected by the living God Himself', he managed to say, 'but what sort of creature are you for I believe that there is more to you than the form which I see before me?' The wolf looked at him with red eyes which glowed menacingly in the firelight.

'As I told you, I am one who lives under a terrible curse', it replied. 'Once I was like you but am now forced to wear this terrible form for a period of seven years. Yet in my heart I am still a devout Christian in need of succour and blessing. And there are yet more of us out in yonder forest who are afflicted with the same curse.' The priest composed himself slightly.

'And yet, you worship God and openly and freely acknowledge the sacrifice of His son for mankind at Calvary?' he enquired. 'You can acknowledge that with all your heart?'

The wolf stretched itself close to the fire and the boy ran back into the shadows and sat there, crouching in terror.

'Aye and gladly', said the creature. 'Although we wear this

ghastly form, we are as human and in need of salvation as any other people.' The priest nodded thoughtfully, his initial terror beginning to fade.

'But how came you by this fearsome form?' he asked in wonder. 'And why must you wear it for seven years?'

The wolf watched him warily.

'I am a member of Clan Allta, a tribe of this region', it answered, 'and like yourself, Father, we are believers in Jesus Christ and in the power of His salvation. However, in times long past, we were cursed for some ancient sin by the blessed Abbot Natalis.'

The priest took in a sharp breath. He had heard of Natalis, who had come to Ireland shortly after the Blessed Patrick to bring the Word of God to a dark and pagan land. He had even read some of the holy man's works. From what he had read, he had always imagined the holy man to be exceedingly severe and inflexible in his teachings and one who would brook no deviation from his own interpretations of God's law.

'The sin which my clan committed has long been forgotten', went on the wolf, 'but the curse is still in force. Every seven years two of us must lose our mortal form to wear the skin of the wild wolf and must live in the deep woods away from the rest of our clan. When the seven years are up we shed our animal form and regain our human shape and two others must take our place. It is a terrible burden, Father, and one which will never be lifted, for Natalis is long dead.

'My wife and I were chosen to take the wolf-shape over six years ago. We were old and it was assumed that the clan could do without us, and so we were driven out from among our people under the curse. Our time in wolf-shape had almost passed when some hunters, passing through these woodlands, aimed an arrow which struck my wife, grievously wounding her. Father, I fear that she is not long for this world and I would implore you to give her the final absolution before she dies.'

The beast looked at the priest with large and imploring eyes. 'She lies in a place not far from here. I beg you, come and minister to her.'

The creature spoke so earnestly and with such passion that the priest could not find it in his heart to refuse.

'Very well', he said, motioning to the boy to remain where he was by the fire. 'Lead me to where your wife lies and if she is truly a Christian, I will administer the final sacraments to her.' At his words, the wolf sprang up and moved to the very edge of the firelight, waiting for the priest to follow.

'Come then', it said. 'We must make haste for I fear that her hour may be passing even as we speak.' Gathering up his religious books, the priest followed and the wolf made off into the darkness of the wood.

The journey deep into the forest was a dangerous one. The wolf moved swiftly and silently ahead of the old man, and the priest was now sure that any noises that had been made earlier were to alert him to the beast's presence near his fire. The trail that they followed was a difficult path, pitted with holes and deep gullies which the priest often found awkward to negotiate. At length they came to a fork in the trail, marked by a lightning-blasted tree. Close by there was a small river flowing and the roots of the ancient oak trailed over into the water.

'Here we are', said the wolf suddenly. The priest squinted in the gloom. There in a small cave among the jumbled roots lay an old she-wolf, as grizzled and thin as her mate. At his approach, she raised her ancient head.

'See, my dear', said the first wolf in a low and soothing voice, 'I have done as I promised and have brought a priest for you.'

Kneeling down, the priest scrambled under the entrance to the cave and squatted beside the she-wolf. There was a great wound on her flank from which part of the shaft of an arrow still stuck out. The priest moved closer to the dying animal.

'Who are you?' he whispered. 'What are you?' The female further lifted her head with some difficulty and blood bubbled between her wolf-lips.

'My husband may have already told you', she answered. 'We are the Werewolves of Ossory, condemned to live in this guise for a season. We are sometimes hunted for our pelts which are extremely valuable and I have been wounded by hunters. I desire to die with the Holy Offices of a priest. Hear my confession and grant me your blessing, Father'. The priest nodded hesitantly.

'You think we are evil', went on the she-wolf. 'You think that this is some trick of the Evil One, sent to lure you away from the sacred paths of the Church.' The priest nodded again. 'Yet we readily acknowledge the name of God, of Jesus Christ His Son and of the Virgin Mary. What creature of evil could do that? I tell you that underneath this fearsome form we are as human and as Christian as yourself, Father.' The priest still seemed uncertain.

'What will it take to convince you?' asked the male wolf, rearing up on its hind-legs. 'If I were to walk like a man would that set your mind at rest that we are truly human?' The priest hesitated. 'We will do anything to convince you, if you will hear my wife's confession!' The priest licked his dry lips uneasily.

'You say that you are human', he answered, 'but ... but I see only the animal. And certainly you speak like mortals and yet your words come in the rough grunts of the beast. If ... if I could but see the human which you say lurks beneath the wolf-skin, then my mind would be at rest.'

The female wolf straightened herself painfully. The priest drew back in alarm but then saw that she did not mean to threaten him.

'Very well', she said. 'In the name of the living God, behold my true face.' And she brought her right forepaw to her jaws and began to gnaw and bite at the skin. Blood spurted out and part of the leg fell away to reveal the fingers of a human hand below. Raising the hand to its belly, the female wolf proceeded to rip and tear at the flesh there, pulling it back and opening it as though it was a hairy garment. The wolf-head seemed to fall away like a woollen mask and, beneath skin and membrane, the priest thought that he saw another, human head. This was the head of an old woman, thin and brown-skinned, narrow and with hair plastered across the sides of the face.

'Jesu!' he muttered, crossing himself. The woman's ancient mouth worked to form words.

'There, Father', said the old lady's voice. 'Now do you believe? Beneath that wolf-body we are indeed human.' She worked and tore through sinew and gristle, allowing her little head to poke out through.

'Now, Father', said the male wolf. 'You have heard our tale, you know that we are human and are true believers. Will you hear my wife's confession and grant her the absolution for which she craves?' The priest sighed at the horror of it all and at the awfulness of the holy curse which lay upon the old couple. Sometimes, he thought, those who called themselves Christian were far worse in their ways than the pagans whom they sought to convert.

'I will hear your confession', he said slowly and with much sadness in his voice. He bent down as the male wolf moved away into the dark, and listened to the small, halting voice as the old woman made her final confession. Then he made the sign of the cross above her.

'I grant you my absolution', he said. 'Go to meet your maker in peace.' The she-wolf sank down into the darkness with a contented sigh.

'Now, though my body dies in its present form', she whispered, 'my immortal soul shall be with God.' And she laid her head down and sank into a deep and restful sleep.

At first light, the male wolf led the priest back to his campsite where the boy was waiting for him. Later, the beast led the two of them to the very edge of the forest so that they could continue their journey. As they were about to depart, the priest turned to the wolf and said:

'Tell me if you know, will the invader remain in Ireland for much longer?' He asked the question for he imagined that the wolf, being a supernatural creature, might have some knowledge of the future. The animal considered for a while.

'On account of the grievous sins of our nation and the enormous wickedness of the people here, God has inflicted the rule of a foreign enemy upon them. As to whether they will remain, I cannot tell at present. Return to these woods upon your way back from Meath and I may be able to tell you.'

And he bid the priest farewell and loped off back into the forest. The priest called after him that he would return with all possible speed to hear the answer but by that time the wolf had returned to the dark woodland depths. Sadly, the priest turned and continued on his journey.

His business in Meath took him much longer than he had expected and so it was early in the following year before he journeyed back to Ulster. On his way, he stopped in the woods of

Ossory but, although he searched, he could not find any sign of the wolf at all. Perhaps he had been killed by hunters or maybe he had moved on. Either way there was not a trace of him to be seen.''

The Black Art

*Although there were few witchcraft trials in Ireland to compare
with those on the Continent or in England, there is no doubt that
witchcraft was practised in remote areas. Country witchcraft was
not the art of grandiose spells and incantations designed to bring
great riches for the sorcerer. Rather, it concerned itself with the
humdrum routine of daily life. Milking cows, churning butter,
baking bread, tending livestock – the normal chores of rural life –
could all be influenced by the dark sciences. People had to be
careful when going about their work and had to take the proper
precautions against supernatural evil before doing so. I have seen
the straw halter which was put around the mouth of the churn
before churning as a protection against "stealing the profits";
otherwise the butter produced through churning might be
magically transported to the churn of a neighbouring witch.*

*Milk, being a staple of any country community, was especially
vulnerable and there are many stories about rural witches, often
in the guise of hares, stoats, cats or some other furtive animal,
creeping through the fields early in the morning in order to suck
the milk from the udders of cattle grazing there. At one time
rabbits, stoats and weasels were common throughout the
countryside and their movements through meadows in the
morning mist probably formed the basis of many old stories
concerning witchcraft. Many of these sightings happened around
May Morning (1 May) and, as this coincided with the ancient
Celtic festival of Beltane (30 April), these events took on an*

added sinister significance.

The following story was told to me by the great Cavan storyteller, Phil Bernard MacDonnell. Phil was well known across Ireland as a travelling musician and claimed to have attended wakes and weddings in every county. He was born and raised in the townland of Moneygashal, County Cavan, and many of the tales which he told were from that area. Sadly, Phil died in April 1995 and many of the old stories went with him. This, however, is an exception.

The Curse of the Hare Woman

"I know that this is a true story for I spoke to the man that it happened to myself. In fact, I was reared in the next townland to him and our families were always very friendly. Michael McCaffrey he was, from Ligillan, over beyond Moneygashal. He was a great huntsman and was always setting traps for foxes and hares. At this time the lands around Moneygashal were thick with wildlife and there were those that made a living out of catching rabbits and selling them for meat. It was safe to eat rabbits in those days before the disease [myxomatosis] came on them; their flesh was as tender as any chicken and they were a great delicacy in many country houses. And hares, too. Their meat is darker and has a more gamey taste but they are just as good to eat.

Anyway, this Michael McCaffrey made his living at catching hares and rabbits in the hills beyond The Black [Blacklion] and he had traps set all through the fields there. The ground up around Moneygashal Rock was thick with their warrens so there was plenty to be had.

This evening he came up to inspect one of these traps away in a

remote part of the hills. He had set it in the shadow of a stone
dyke, close to a break in the stones where the hares and rabbits
would be coming through. And when he got up to it, there was a
hare caught in it as neatly as you please, struggling hard to get
out. Every time that he went to free it, it wriggled away from him
very awkwardly and he couldn't let it loose and put it into his
bag. He was sure that the poor creature was hurting itself with
all its contortions and he felt for it, for he was a very good man
at heart.

'Hold still', says he to it, in a kindly tone. 'If you stay where
you are I can set you free and you won't have to hurt yourself by
wriggling about.'

Hardly were the words out of his mouth than the shape of the
hare seemed to shift and change before his eyes. The hairy skin
seemed to slough away and fall to nothing and the body
appeared to stretch upwards until it was nearly as tall as Michael
McCaffrey himself. The face of the creature moved and melted in
front of him and he found himself looking at a lovely young
woman, cowering in a niche in the stone dyke. By the shape of
her face and the build of her, he knew her to be one of the
McManus's that lived away about Gowland but he didn't know
exactly who she was. She looked at him for a minute.

'Who are you?' says he, very frightened. The woman gave a
sort of half-smile.

'I am the hare that you caught', says she. 'I was changed into
that shape long ago by a witch-woman that once lived in this
district. A powerful and very evil magician she was altogether,
and one who secretly practised the black art against her
neighbours when the fancy took her. She turned me into a hare
because of some disagreement that I had with her and I was
condemned to remain in that form until someone spoke to me

directly and offered me a kindness. You have done so and have released me, for which I thank you. But you must now escort me home to my people for I have been away from them for a long time.'

So he threw his coat about her shoulders and led her down towards Moneygashal. She looked around her and saw the houses down in the valley below and she remarked that everything was changed. She mentioned people that she knew but of whom Michael McCaffrey had never heard. He remembered his grandmother talking about some of the names that the strange woman spoke of but that was a long time in the past and those people had been dead for many years.

Then he recalled an old tale that had been told in the countryside long ago about a girl of the McManus's who had vanished way beyond Moneygashal seventy or more years before. She had gone out one morning and had never returned and though her family had looked for her for long years after, not a trace of her had ever been found. This must indeed be the very woman, he thought.

He looked at her closely and noticed that, with every step she took, she seemed to grow slightly older. Her black, flowing hair became streaked with grey and began to thin, her face became hard and narrow, marked with lines and crow's feet; her back became more and more bent as they went down the hill. Instead of the beautiful young woman that had been cowering by the wall, Michael McCaffrey found himself walking beside a raddled old hag who hobbled a few steps behind him. It was as if all the seventy years were catching up with her in the space of a few moments as she rapidly turned into an old and hideous crone.

He crossed himself and drew back but the ancient woman walked on, growing ever older with every step that she took. At last, she was nothing more than a horrid skeleton over which the skin was thinly stretched like a fine, dry parchment. The horrible thing tried to speak but it made only a hoarse, rattling sound that was somewhere between a cough and a croak. She took another step towards him and her whole frame seemed to fall in on itself, dissolving into a grey dust which the wind caught and blew away before Michael could do anything.

In a few moments the hare-woman was gone, wafted away across the fields on the wind, and he saw her no more. The coat which he had put round her shoulders fluttered to the ground. Recovering slightly from the horror of it all, he called on the Holy Name to protect himself from evil and then hurried down to the houses at Moneygashal and told them what had happened. But he could show no evidence of the occurrence and the people around that area wouldn't believe him.

I do believe the story, for he was a very decent man – not given to telling lies – and, anyway, what motive would he have for telling a story like that? There are more people who practise the black art in the country places than you would imagine."

The hare was a symbol of evil in many country areas. This may be attributed to its pagan significance: it was the symbol of the Celtic moon-goddess and was closely allied with the witchcraft and wonder-working which was traditionally carried out by moonlight. The memory of that tradition may well have lingered on in the minds of rural people. As early as the twelfth century, Giraldus Cambrensis wrote about certain old Irish women who could transform themselves into the guise of hares for the purposes of working evil.

The following tale also uses the hare motif to symbolise evil, with the figure of the tailor representing good. Tailors, like blacksmiths, were important individuals in any rural community, and were often credited with special powers against evil. Although this version of the story comes from County Sligo, the tale is well-known in many parts of Ireland.

The Tailor and the Hare Woman

"There was a tailor one time, travelled all over Ireland as tailors used to do in the days long ago. He would come into a place and would set up in a local house and the people all around would bring him things to mend. That was always the way of it in country areas.

Now, this tailor was coming through County Sligo and he had always taken lodgings with a farmer and his wife that lived near Coole. He slept in a small back room at the gable end of the house, just above the kitchen, and used a back scullery to do his tailoring, paying the couple a little bit of rent for the space. The farmer was a very old man but the wife was young and wicked-looking and the tailor was wary of her. However, she was always very civil to him and he thought that he was wrong to doubt her.

One day, he arrived at the house to find that the farmer had died a good number of months before but that the wife was still living there. She made him very welcome and told him that he could continue to lodge there for as long as he wanted and at the same rent. The tailor was now very sure that he had misjudged the woman and that she was decent enough. Indeed, she was so good to him that she told him to lie as long as he wanted in the morning and that she would bring him his breakfast. He thought that this was very fair and thanked the woman kindly. All the same, he noticed that, when she spoke, her tone was gentle but her eyes were as hard as metal. Still, he had been travelling for some time and resolved to take her at her word and have a lie-in for the first few days of his lodging there.

The next morning, however, he was awake with the first sun of the day. So as not to disturb the woman of the house he lay in bed for a while. He could hear her moving about in the kitchen below and, for a moment, he thought that he heard water splashing but he couldn't be sure. After a long while she came up and brought him his breakfast and told him to lie a little while longer. So he did, and got up feeling very refreshed.

The following morning he was awake at the same time and, this time, he was sure that he heard movement and the sound of water in the kitchen below him. Wondering what was going on, he got up and crept quietly down the stairs so as not to disturb the woman. Looking round the kitchen door, he saw her filling a big wooden tub with water. She looked like she might be going to take a bath, so the tailor made to turn on his heel and creep back to bed. Suddenly, she peeled off all her clothes and leapt into the water. There was a flash and a puff of smoke and a great big hare jumped out of the tub and through the open kitchen door, out into the morning.

The tailor was dumbstruck and very frightened for he knew what had happened and what his hostess was about so early in the morning. The woman was a witch and she had turned herself into a hare in order to go out into the morning and do mischief to her neighbours. In some places, witches went about in the guise of small animals, sucking milk from the teats of grazing cattle so that they were dry and would give nothing when they came to be milked. Sometimes the witch in her animal form would jump into a baby's cradle when it was sleeping and smother the infant. Witches were always getting up to terrible evil like that in the countryside.

Well, the tailor was greatly frightened and would have left the place then and there but he had a good number of sewing jobs that day and, anyway, he was possessed of a great curiosity and wanted to see exactly what the woman was up to. He went back to bed and, after a long time, she came back again and brought him up his breakfast, wishing him a 'Good morning' as she did so, as if she had just risen herself.

The next morning, he was wide awake from well before light and was determined to creep down and see what he could see. As soon as the sun was coming up, he could hear the noises again in the kitchen below him and, listening hard, the sound of water being carried into the kitchen. Getting up, he crept down and peered around the door. The woman had now the wooden tub filled and was peeling off her clothes. Not knowing that she was being watched, she leapt into the bath. In her place, out jumped the large hare. Without looking around, it was out through the kitchen door and away across the fields.

Quick as a flash and without thinking of the possible danger, the tailor undressed himself, ran into the kitchen and jumped into the water. As I said, he was cursed with a great curiosity and he wanted to see what the hare-woman was doing and where she was going. As soon as he touched the water, there was a flash and a puff of smoke and he was transformed into a hare himself. Then he leapt out of the bath and followed the witch out through the kitchen door and over the fields.

On and on they ran, across wide fields and across sheughs, hedges and ditches. All the while the witch-woman kept well ahead of the tailor, but he was still able to see her and follow her wherever she went. At length they came to a small, grassy hill in the middle of the townland of Ballylee, and there a good number of other hares had gathered. There were big hares and small hares, black hares and brown hares, hares with only one ear and hares that had strangely marked coats. They had formed themselves into a circle on top of the little hill. The tailor knew instantly that these were the witches of the locality and that they had gathered here so that they could work their evil in the district together. Quietly and without fuss he joined their company.

A big, grey buck-hare with a dark patch on its back stood up in the centre of the circle and spoke to all the witches that were gathered about him.

'Go home!' says he to them, 'For we'll do no bad work here today. There is a stranger amongst us!' And all the other hares turned around and looked in the direction of the tailor. He knew then that he had been found out! The hare that was the witch-woman with whom he was lodging opened her mouth and issued a long and terrible shriek and with that the tailor knew that he had to get home and transformed back or something awful would befall him. He took to his heels and fled across the fields towards Coole and the bath of magic water. But the witch-woman was not far behind him.

Faster and faster he ran but she stayed on his tail and indeed she seemed to be gaining on him. Back through the sheughs and hedges he ran and down along loanings and boreens, back towards the farmhouse. As he neared the gate of her yard he chanced a look behind him and saw that she was indeed very close. He ran across the yard and in through the still-open kitchen door. With a flying jump, he sprang into the water and it closed over him. In an instant, he was transformed again and was back into his own true shape. However, even as he changed back, the witch-woman came through the door and made a leap herself for the enchanted water in the tub.

Grabbing his clothes, which lay in a heap beside the tub, the tailor made a run across the kitchen and up the stairs. He looked back as he did so and saw that the witch-woman had also changed back into her own shape and was coming after him, letting out terrible yells. There was a knife lying on the kitchen table and she grabbed that and came on, waving it threateningly.

The tailor got to his bedroom and managed to shut and secure the door after him. He held it closed while the witch-woman hammered on it and screamed awful threats and oaths against him. Gathering together his bits and pieces, he opened the small window in the gable-end of the room and let himself through it, dropping down into the yard below as quick as he could. And all the while, he could hear the witch-woman beating and breaking at the door.

He ran and ran across the countryside and never stopped until he was on the outskirts of Sligo town itself. He had left his thimble and several pieces of stuff behind him, but nothing in God's own creation would make him go back for them. He took up tailoring again but he never struck out on the road towards Coole. He never knew what became of the witch-woman, nor did he want to find out, for those that traffic in the dark sciences are best left alone.

However, some time after, he was working in a country house, doing some sewing by the light of a lamp, and he had to bend over the cloth that he was mending so that he could see it better. One of the children who was playing about the floor looked queerly at him and, climbing up beside him, said:

'What is that on the back of your neck, sir?'

The tailor put up his hand and felt along the back of his neck. To his great horror, there was a ring of coarse fur, the same as you would find around the neck of a hare! It was a part of him that the enchanted water hadn't touched when he was in his hare form and which hadn't been transformed back. That ring of fur stayed with him until the day that he died and he had to wear a scarf, even on a warm day, to keep curious folk from staring at it or asking him about it.

So if you ever see a woman taking a bath in a wooden tub before the first light of morning or a tailor with a scarf about his shoulders on a hot summer's day, then you'll know for certain that my story is true."

Not all witches in the countryside used their powers for evil. Some were local wise women with a knowledge of herbs and potions which they used for various purposes, usually to heal sickness, cure pain, or as charms to instil love, induce children or bring about good luck. Several of these "hedge witches" or "fairy doctors" enjoyed a great reputation far beyond the borders of their own townland or their own county. Moll Anthony from the Red Hills in County Kildare, for example, was well known as a healer even in the North of Ireland, as was Maurice Griffin, the "fairy doctor" of County Kerry who, it was rumoured, got his strange powers from a magical cloud which had drifted across some land upon which he was working.

The most famous of all the country witches, however, was the notorious Biddy Early, the wise-woman of County Clare. Biddy's name was well-known as a healer and many people travelled from all over Ireland to her lonely cottage on the shores of Kilbarron Lake. Many stories are told about her and about her strange and mysterious powers.

Biddy Early

"I'm sure that you have heard about Biddy Early from Clare. There are some that will tell you that she was nothing more than a wise-woman – a harmless soul – but the clergy always said that she was a witch and that she dealt with ghosts and fairies.

She had a dark glass bottle somewhere in her house that they said was the source of all her magic. Some say that she won it in a wager through playing cards with a fairy man but I heard that she had been married four times and it was the ghost of one of her husbands, Tom Flannery of Carrowroe, that had given it to her. He had come back from the other world and had brought it with him. Once she had that she could do wonderful things and could foretell the future and heal people.

But the priests were greatly against her, for she never went to mass and she had married men who were younger than herself without the benefit of the clergy. They said that she had put the glamour (a spell) on these young men and maybe there was something in that for all her husbands died before her. They said that there wasn't a man over forty years of age in the countryside that hadn't been with her at one time or another.

There was one priest in particular, the curate in Feakle, who spoke out against her very sharply. Then one day he was passing by her house and she came to the door and threw something against the flanks of his horse that made the animal bolt into the middle of a river and it wouldn't go back nor forwards. The priest just had to sit there until Biddy came down and lifted the spell and the horse continued on across the river. You can be sure that he never spoke out against her after that.

And there was a man from Tulla who travelled up to Kilbarron to see her about his wife who was lying sick with a fever. Biddy

Early told him that there was nothing that she herself could do for him.

'But', says she, 'in four days time, a disgraced priest will call at your house. And if you give him a crust of bread he will cure your wife for you.' And she sent him home again.

In four days' time, a travelling man called at his door, asking for a crust of bread. It turned out that he was a disgraced priest – one Father Shannon – who had been defrocked for drunkenness and brawling. The man brought him in and he cured his wife with a touch, as Biddy Early had foreseen. Ah, but she had great powers indeed!

Anyway, the story that I am going to tell you concerns an old man called Dillane, who went up to Kilbarron to find out what had happened to his daughter. She had left home almost a year before and hadn't been heard of since. There was talk amongst his neighbours that she had run off with a tinker-boy that had come through the district some time before but old Dillane wasn't so sure. He went to Biddy Early, together with a couple of his sons, to see if she could help, for she could see things that other mortals couldn't.

It was a very wet day when they went to see her, full of sleet and rain, and they were fairly soaked when they reached Kilbarron. Now at this time Biddy Early was married to a man called Tommy Feeny and when Dillane and his sons came in, soaking wet, she says to her husband:

'Tommy, go to the back of the kitchen and bring a bottle and give them all a drop.'

And he went and brought them all a glass of poteen and they drunk it down. But Biddy Early herself would only drink gin.

When she heard what Dillane wanted, she nodded her head as though she knew all about it.

'Your daughter has not left the country at all', she said, 'and if you have a mind to see her, you should go down to the old field-road that runs through Thomas Crone's lands at Ballinabuckey, down towards Cloughreeve, in three days' time. Go at midday and you will see her going along in front of you. But do not try to speak to her for she is with the Gentlemen [fairies] and you will only bring down ill-fortune on yourself if you attempt to interfere.'

Well, it was just as she had said. Dillane went up to the field-road in Ballinabuckey three days later and walked along it at midday. When he looked around him, there was his daughter's pattern [spectre] going along, a little ways in front of him. He walked more quickly to try and catch up with it but no matter how hard he walked, it always kept a bit in front of him.

About halfway along the field-road there was a small lake, lying in a hollow of the hills, and it was here that the girl left the path and turned down, as if to the water's edge. She walked straight towards the rim of the lake and seemed just about to walk into it. Believing that he was losing her forever, Dillane cried out:

'Oh, come back to me! Don't go into the water!' Whereupon the pattern turned and looked at him with eyes that were already dead and with a face as pale as snow. Then the shape vanished into the lake, just like smoke across its surface, and he saw her no more.

Stricken with grief, Dillane went back up to Kilbarron to see Biddy Early and to ask her what the awful vision meant. The old woman sipped at her drink for a long time without speaking and when she did speak her voice was low and sad:

'It is as I thought', she said, with a great weight in her words. 'Your daughter is lying at the bottom of that lake. She was drowned by one of the Crones because she would not go with him. But, because she was so cruelly murdered, the Gentlemen have taken her for their own and her pattern walks the field road at certain times of the day. Tell me, did you speak to it?' And Dillane told her that he had cried out and that the pattern had turned its head to look at him. Biddy Early shook her head sadly.

'Ochone for you', she sighed. 'You may go home now for there is nothing more that I can do for you. Had you not spoken I might have been able to do something but, since you have done so, you have brought the wrath of the Gentry on you. Go home and see your family right away for you are not long for this world.' And she took another swallow of her drink and would say no more.

With a heavy heart, Old Dillane climbed into his cart and headed home. He lived only two days more. They found him dead in bed, killed by a stroke, just as Biddy Early had foretold. I heard that they drained the lake over in Ballinabuckey and that they found the remains of a girl in it, but she had been in the water for so long that the police couldn't positively identify her and nobody was ever charged.

But Biddy Early had foreseen it all. She had always great powers to see the future."

Great and Fighting Men

Ancient heroes have always loomed large in Irish folklore. Stories and legends of great heroes in times gone by stand, like ancient stones, against the background of more formal history. Since much of the tradition was oral it is not surprising that such tales survive, handed down from one generation to the next, to awe and enchant the listener.

In these old tales, too, there is an attempt to connect past to present. The heroes of old are not really dead, for example, they are simply sleeping, waiting for someone to wake them or for some awful doom to befall Ireland, when they will rise again to defend its shores. From time to time, people will accidentally stumble across these slumbering warriors and may have some passing encounter with them, then send them back to sleep once more.

Of course, the myth of sleeping warriors is not unique to Ireland nor to Irish heroes. King Arthur and his knights sleep beneath St Michael's Mount, for example, whilst Vlad Tepes (Vlad the Impaler) slumbers beneath the monastery at Snagov in Transylvania in Eastern Europe. Both wait for a time when their country is in peril so that they may rise again to defend it. However, the misty Irish countryside often gives such stories a greater immediacy and potency. It is as if one expects these old warriors to come riding out of the mist and into the present day. Which, of course, in some of these old stories they actually do, as in the following tale from County Fermanagh.

Donn Binn Maguire and the Coppal Bawn

The land along the Fermanagh border, to the south-west of Enniskillen, is lonely and wild. It is mostly mountain, lake and bog, dotted here and there with small villages and hamlets tucked away around some bend of a road – Belcoo, Garrison, Derrygonnelly. Here, the mist rolls back and forth across a bleak but beautiful landscape, lingering in the hollows and making strange and terrible shapes out of ancient standing stones. The region is famous for its caves and potholes, drawing explorers to places such as the Marble Arch and Boho, where there are many deep and still unfathomed caverns. There is talk too, in the tales of the area, that these caverns are doorways to strange, underground kingdoms where the Good People, or fairies, may still dwell. From time to time, people have been lost in such places and it is a common belief that they have been "carried away" to the dark realms below.

A great range of limestone mountains extends throughout this region, stretching away towards Sligo in the west. The most easterly of these is called Binaughlin, towering above the houses which make up the hamlets of Florencecourt and Swanlinbar. Many mountains in this area have legends connected with them and Binaughlin is no exception. Long ago, it is said, a famous chieftain was carried away by the Good People and made a prisoner under the mountain itself. The story is well-known amongst the old people of the region, and on a stormy night you may meet an old man, seated by the roaring fire in Frank Eddy Maguire's public house in Blacklion, who will draw his chair nearer to the blaze, fill his pipe and begin to relate the tale of Donn Binn Maguire:

"You will have heard of him no doubt? No? Oh, a great chieftain he was, the fiercest and proudest of all the chieftains in ancient Fermanagh. Now, what I'm telling you happened long ago in the old and barbarous times when the Maguires and the O'Rourkes fought in all the lands around the Hanging Rock and across the islands of Inishee and Cushrush on Lough Macnean. Bad, bloody and pagan times they were and I pray that they never come to the county of Fermanagh again.

They said that whenever this Donn Binn rode out to battle, that he rode like the wind and fought like fury and there were none who could keep up with him or who could stand against him. He was a grand and handsome man altogether and it is said that no woman could resist him whenever she had looked upon him.

Also, the Good People that lived in Binaughlin Mountain had set their eyes at him, for they have always designs on the mortal kind and will try to carry them away to their own dark country at the first opportunity. This is the way that it was with Donn Binn Maguire and the way that it came about was like this:

Donn Binn had a great love of horses. It was even said about him that he loved the saddle so much that he would only put his foot to the earth when he had no other choice. He had many beautiful and powerful steeds quartered in the stables at his castle and he always boasted that no man in Ireland had horses that were better than his. His stallions, he said, were the strongest and swiftest in all the lands around. There were none who could touch them.

There was a great rivalry at this time between the O'Rourkes and the Maguires to see who had the best of everything and the O'Rourkes put it about, as a challenge, that one of their chieftains had bought a magnificent stallion from an Arab man.

This horse, they said, had no equal in Ireland let alone in Fermanagh.

'Now', says they, 'for all his boasting, there is none to equal it in the stables of Donn Binn Maguire.'

When Donn Binn heard this, he was very much angered for he was a quick-tempered man and was easily drawn into a dispute. He vowed that if this horse of the O'Rourkes was indeed the finest in Ireland, he would find and own the greatest stallion in the world!

Now in those days there were great herds of wild horses all across the high hills of Fermanagh and all through the Iron Mountains into Sligo and Cavan as well, and it was great sport amongst the princes and chieftains of Ulster to ride out and catch some of them. Many's a fine stallion which graced a chieftain's stables had been cut from the wild herds which roamed up among the high mountain places. The finest of all these horses were supposed to be found on the upper slopes of Binaughlin Mountain itself.

Anyway, Donn Binn Maguire and his horsemen came riding through Florencecourt and Swanlinbar and over Binaughlin Mountain on a grand hunt. They passed through at a time of the year when the country people were burning the gorse on the mountainside to clear the land for sheep and it was said in all the villages through which they passed that Donn Binn was looking for the wild horses which were supposed to gather on Binaughlin's upper slopes. It was also said that he would not be turned until he had found them.

And find them he did, for no sooner had they reached a place high up on the mountain when the chieftain saw, grazing in a hollow in front of him, the finest and sturdiest-looking white steed that he had ever laid eyes on. Its skin was like the unspoiled snow and it had great muscles which rippled like the wind as it grazed. Donn Binn, who was a great judge of horses, instantly knew that this was a special steed.

'Faith', says he, 'but I will have that horse for my own! If that were in my stables, it would surely quieten the crowing of the O'Rourkes and I would be the envy of every prince in Fermanagh, and in all of Ireland too!'

His followers looked around them but they could see nothing, only the white mist trailing across the slopes of Binaughlin Mountain and the grey-backed crows lighting on and taking off again from the rocky ground. They saw no horse at all, and thought that their master must either be mad or bewitched.

Donn Binn Maguire was bewitched all right for it was no natural horse that he saw, but a supernatural creature sent by the Good People (may their heels be turned towards us this day!) to lure him away from the world of men and into their thrall!

Not knowing this, Donn Binn called his men and swore a great oath that he would ride after this grand horse and capture it, should he have to follow it across all the lands of Fermanagh. He instructed them that they could keep up with him if they had a mind to but that he would not wait for them if they fell behind. He would have that horse at all costs! The servants looked at each other in amazement and whispered amongst themselves for, no matter how hard they looked, they could still see no horse.

'Look!' said Donn Binn to one of them. He spoke softly so as not to alarm the horse which, so far, had paid them no heed. 'Do you not see it grazing over yonder in the shadow of that great rock? Do you not see the rise and fall of its great head as it grazes?' But the servant only shook his head.

'In truth, Master', says he, 'I see only the shadows of the clouds moving across the mountain!' Angry at having his word doubted by his own servants, Donn Binn called another of his men to him.

'Do you not see it?' he asked, pointing. 'It is eating the tender young grasses down in yon' hollow! Do you not see where it goes as it moves from clump to clump?' But the servant only shrugged his shoulders.

'In truth, Master', says he, 'I see only smoke from the gorse fires further along the mountain!' Donn Binn's anger rose in the back of his throat like a black and bitter bile. He called yet another man to him and pointed to the hollow.

'See! The steed senses that we are here', he hissed. 'Do you not see him lift his mighty head to sniff at the breeze for our scent?' But the servant only looked around him.

'In truth, Master', he answered, 'I see only the wind ruffling the tufts of the wild mountain heather. I can see no horse at all!'

Much angered by their replies, Donn Binn Maguire swore a mighty oath and, digging his heels into the flanks of his horse, he thundered off after the fine white stallion in the hollow below.

Sensing his approach, the creature reared on its hind legs and suddenly took off like a startled bird across a meadow, with the chieftain after it at full gallop. Donn Binn rode like the wind in order to claim his prize and, though his men struggled to keep up with him, they soon fell far behind and he was lost to their sight. It was an enchantment of the Good People.

Well, far across the slopes of Binaughlin Mountain rode Donn Binn Maguire, following the enchanted stallion. He galloped hard over rocks and down streams, through briars and across lintholes and bogs. He galloped until he and his own horse were bathed in sweat and gasping for the want of wind. But never once did he overtake the magical horse which kept as far ahead of him as ever. They travelled far beyond the places where any person could live and galloped across lands that were nothing but bare mountain rock and which were peopled only by the crows and starlings. They galloped across places that were thick with purple heather and where only the wild hares started up at their approach.

At length they came to a very remote and lonely place, near to the very summit of the mountain itself. There, set deep into a stone cliff, the mouth of a great cave yawned, very wide and pitch black as night. A cold wind blew directly from it, away across the mountainside, fairly chilling the air all about. Another horse would have been frightened and turned there but the white stallion never broke its stride and plunged straight into the darkness with Donn Binn Maguire hard upon its heels. This was all as the Good People had planned.

With the sun now behind him, the chieftain found himself at the head of a narrow, cold, rocky passageway which seemed to lead down into the very depths of Binaughlin itself. The strange steed didn't hesitate for one moment, but rushed onwards through the gloom, the sound of its feet ringing loudly against the echoing rock. Donn Binn Maguire was fearless and the enchantment of the Good People was upon him. Urging his own horse on, he too rushed down the passage into the dark.

Down, down into the depths of the mountain and into the realm of the Good People themselves went the chase. Several times, the chieftain tried to overtake the white stallion but it always stayed ahead of him in the narrow passageway which led through the rock.

Suddenly, the passage that he had been following came to an end and Donn Binn Maguire found himself on the shores of a vast underground lake, stretching away through a mighty cavern ahead of him. The whole place was illuminated only by the dim glow from the eerie, cold mosses which hung from the walls all around. On the edge of this huge and tideless sea, the magic horse stopped, the enchantment was lifted from Donn Binn and he knew instantly that he was in some dreadful underground land, far away from his own folk. He realised too, that this was the very edge of the gloomy country of the Good People, deep below the earth itself, and that beyond the vast cavern-sea, kings and princes that were not of this world had their castles and dwellings.

Very frightened, he turned his horse to try to escape but the passageway down which he had come quickly and magically closed in upon itself, sealing him far beneath Binaughlin Mountain. He stayed on the shore of that strange underground sea until the Good People themselves came across that mighty water in their boats, all hung with lanterns, to carry him back to their forts, deep in that continuing gloom.

I've heard it said that his men waited the length of three days for him to return but, when there was no sign of him, they returned to his castle in great distress. It was put about in the countryside that he had been killed by the O'Rourkes who were raiding all through Fermanagh at that time, and that his body had been lost in a bog.

Time went by. Months turned into years and the years into centuries. Donn Binn Maguire lived amongst the Good People under Binaughlin Mountain until his name was all but forgotten. In all that time, however, he never died for death has no claim on the fairy kind or on those that live with them. The Good People were kind to him and treated him well, for they are not always as evil as some would have you believe, and he became a great prince among them, just as he had been before in his own lands in Fermanagh. They tended to his every want and fed him on their own food so that he was never hungry. Their meat, I am told, is the same as human food, only it has less nourishment and is not as satisfying to mortal men.

Gradually, as the years and then the centuries slipped by, he wasted away to a shadow of his former self but still he did not die like any other mortal. Away from the heat and the goodness of the sun, he became as thin as a stick, his skin became as pale as milk and his eyes were as brightly inflamed as the reddest of rubies. In this ill-lit world, he was serenaded and soothed by the music of magical pipes and harps. He was given fine clothes to wear, all of which were made from the richest silks and brocades of the *sidhe* (fairies). He reclined upon a bed of the softest linens and damasks whilst servants carried him all the foodstuffs that he could wish for. And still all this grand living never put meat upon his bones.

He missed the wind on his face; he missed the hunts across the hills of the upper world; the smell of the turf fires and the roar of pleasant human company. The lands of the Good People are dark and dreary – endless, echoing and poorly-lit caverns and deep lakes, and great pits which fall down through unimaginable depths to the very core of the world. God's holy daylight never touches that dark place nor does the wind blow across it. There is no sport or feasting there, nor is there laughter of any description, for the Good People are great sorcerers and take themselves very seriously. Donn Binn was fading away for want of the rowdy company of his own people that he had always enjoyed in Fermanagh.

In the end, he became so miserable that the fairies granted him a special dispensation for, despite all their fearsome magics, they can be kindly when the mood takes them. He would be allowed to return to the lands of Fermanagh at certain times of the year, when the mists hung low over the summit of Binaughlin; but he must always return to the underground realm after the space of a night. Each time, he could take away one person from the mortal world to live with him in his dark kingdom under the earth.

And so it has always been. When the clouds hang low over Binaughlin Mountain, Donn Binn Maguire rides out on a white stallion – the very horse that he had chased into the country of the Good People in the first place – and he will carry away the best-looking girl, the strongest boy or the greatest scholar in the district round about. He takes them back with him to his own lightless world and they are seen no more. It is said that he travels across the mountain slopes most especially on May Eve or on Halloweve Night but also sometimes on some of the other old feasts of seasons that they observe throughout the countryside. Only a piece of mountain ash tied to your chimney or hung above your door will protect a house against him for ash will always turn the fairies. They say, too, that he will never pass by when church bells are ringing for the sound of a bell rung in a holy steeple is a great protection against witches and the *sidhe*.

At night, when all the family is gathered in about the fire and there is much joviality in the house, look quickly to the window for there you may see the pale, lonely face of Donn Binn Maguire peering in with a strange and wistful stare. Then you will know that your son or daughter has been marked by the Good People and will be gone from you before the month is out. It is always like that.

I heard it said, too, that the horse on which the fairy prince rides is a very magical steed. At certain times of the year, it had the power of human speech and could foresee the future. In the olden times, it was called the Coppal Bawn by the people round Binaughlin because of its great beauty. A powerful sort of horse it was altogether.

The old folks said that, years ago, the country people around Florencecourt, Swanlinbar and Wheathill would gather on the top of the mountain and the horse would appear to them and would speak oracles and give out prophesies. To honour it, they carved its shape in the limestone on the side of the mountain and I believe that you can still see the faint trace of it, although it is now very much overgrown. They say that there are horses carved on the hills of England as well but there are none that were ever so beautiful as the Coppal Bawn."

Whilst Donn Binn Maguire was able to ride out of his underground realm from time to time, other mighty heroes of former times remained far below the surface of the earth, locked in a perpetual enchanted slumber, waiting for some summons to return to the sunlit world again. Occasionally, humans might accidentally stumble into their abode and might disturb their sleep of ages. Stories of such intrusions stretch all the way from Rathlin Island (where Robert the Bruce lies sleeping) to Kerry (where Brian Boru might be disturbed) or, indeed, to County Clare:

The Sleeping Warriors

Arguably no place in Ireland is as strange and eerie as the Burren of County Clare. The name Burren comes from the Gaelic *bhoireann*, meaning "rocky place", and there is no other landscape like it in Europe. In parts of it the country takes on the quality of a lunar surface – vast areas of moss-covered limestone, thick with strange flowers and fauna, matched by great fists of rock rising out of the calcified surface as if to threaten the unwary traveller. This is also a land of druid stones, ancient forts, the ivy-clad tower-houses of long-vanished families and of deserted villages and overgrown roads. It is indeed a lonely and sinister place.

Because the Burren is composed of sedimentary rock, water comes and goes through it, creating deep caves and fissures in its surface. There is a belief that they are the portals to the dark fairy world, near which ancient heroes slumber on their sentry duty. But let the interloper beware, for the slightest sound may stir them into action. Indeed, there are many local tales concerning those who have been so ill-advised as to trespass on their domain ....

"They say that there is a cave out on the Burren that only opens once in every seven years. Some would tell you that there is a grand treasure hidden there but that it is unwise to enter it for it is the abode of the fairies and the gold rightfully belongs to them. It is as well to leave it alone.

There was a man named MacMahon, a poacher, that lived over beyond in Ballynalackin and he was out hunting very early one morning, near the old castle there, when he came upon the entrance to a cave that he hadn't noticed before. He had been chasing hares across the rocks when they had suddenly disappeared and, under a rocky overhang, he came upon the mouth of a tunnel, nearly hidden by long grasses. Now he was a curious man and, as he knew the locality well and had never seen this cave-mouth before, he was anxious to know where it went. He had heard old stories of hidden treasures far below the Burren and thought that there might be a lost fortune to be found if he were to explore further.

So, winding long grasses and dry hay into several crude torches which he was able to light with a bit of flint from his tinderbox, he went down into the cave and far beyond the clear daylight. The cave extended back into the rock, like a kind of passage, and MacMahon noticed that its walls seemed to be hung with ancient weaponry, partly gone to rust, and ancient shields marked with a long-vanished heraldry. The place was obviously very old indeed and a voice in the back of his mind told him to turn about and run. Yet both greed and curiosity overcame the warning. If the cavern was indeed very old, he reasoned, then it was quite possible that there would be a treasure of some sort near at hand.

He waded across a small stream which flowed down through the passageway and crouched down to pass below a rocky overhang as he travelled on into the gloom. Not even his improvised torch gave him much light in this underground world. Squeezing through a narrow section of the rock, he suddenly found himself in a high vaulted chamber where stalactites hung down from the parts of the roof that he could actually see. As for the rest of the ceiling, it vaulted away upwards into the dark and was lost to view. The whole place suggested the style of some old hall or burial crypt of some mighty church. Holding up the last of the torches, which was already threatening to burn down, MacMahon examined the rocky walls around him, still convinced that treasure lay in the furthest recesses of the place.

He found no fortune but he saw that the walls were black with soot, as if several fires had been lit against them. Here and there, bits of old armour and abandoned weapons had been scattered across the floor and lay in rough heaps close to the wall. Further along, he found a couple of ancient and primitive fireplaces where charred wood still lay, though it had been cold for a long time. How the smoke had escaped through the shadowy roof he couldn't tell, but it was evident that fires had burned there in times long past.

Then, half-way up the wall, resting in a large niche in the rock, he saw a large silver horn. It was long and curved and appeared to be carved with antique hunting and battle scenes. It lay almost beyond his grasp and, as he stretched up to take it down, MacMahon suddenly became aware that he was not alone in the cavern.

Although his torch had all but expired, his eyes had become accustomed to the gloom and a strange light seemed to glow from a kind of fungus which grew along the rocky walls. He turned around quickly and was amazed to see several figures lying stretched on the ground close to a pile of ancient weaponry, covered with furs and animal pelts. Massive double-headed axes and halberds lay within easy reach of them and, for a second, MacMahon thought that they were dead and that he had blundered into some prehistoric mausoleum, the grave of a Celtic king and his attendants.

As he gazed at them, he realised that they were in fact sleeping, for their chests rose in a strange, regular motion and he heard their deep, steady breathing. He paid them little attention, for their sleep seemed very sound, and turned his thoughts back to the silver horn. It was a fabulous thing and, by stretching a little more, he was able to seize it and lift it down. Standing in the gloom of the cavern, he imagined it even more valuable than he had at first thought, and wondered who had fashioned it and what it might sound like. It had clearly been designed for a man of larger proportions than an ordinary mortal. He was tempted to raise it to his lips and blow, yet heard a warning voice in the back of his head: 'Take care, foolish fellow! Beware!'

But MacMahon was a stubborn man and, dismissing the threat, raised the horn to his lips and gave a blow. He could hardly produce a sound. It made but a tiny noise like the faint sqawk of a goose. Even so, it seemed enough to trouble one of the sleepers for, with a groan, he stirred in his slumber and stretched himself slightly.

'Is it time yet?' he asked, in a voice that was deep and gruff and which clearly had been unused to human speech for a long time. He made to rise and, in the dim light of the wall mosses, MacMahon saw that he was an ancient giant, clad in chain-mail armour and with a great horned helmet on his head. With a shudder, the poacher realised that he had stumbled into the resting place of a band of ancient warriors – perhaps even the great Fionn MacCumhaill and his men – who were deep in enchanted slumber. The sound of the horn – low though it had been – had broken that sleep. His heart was fairly stopping within him but, in a trembling voice, he answered:

'No, it's not time yet. Go back to sleep!'

Now, given the situation, he had displayed a surprising presence of mind. But the ancient warrior was persistent. Hoisting himself up onto one knee, he gripped the shaft of a rusted spear and looked out from under his helmet with red and glittering eyes.

'Then why have you disturbed our sleep?' he asked in hollow, ringing tones which reverberated from the rocky walls round about. To his increasing terror, MacMahon noticed that several of the other sleepers were now beginning to stir and he saw an ancient hand reach for a fallen sword lying nearby. Dragging himself up to his full height, the soldier took an awkward step forward. With a cry born out of pure horror, MacMahon dropped the horn and ran back towards the entrance to the cavern. With a throaty roar, all the warriors now began to stir and to stumble unsteadily to their feet. MacMahon ran along the dark rock passage, conscious of the horrid throng which followed him, gasping and leaping until he at last reached the cave entrance through which he had come.

Once on the upper earth of the Burren, he fell exhausted to the ground whilst, behind him, the entrance closed with a sound like the clap of thunder. When he looked down at the arm which had held the horn, he found it withered, and it remained so until the day he died. But he had had a lucky escape and never more did he go poaching in the Burren close to Ballynalackin Castle. Who knows but those old soldiers are still sleeping somewhere out there."

Not only do these old stories tell of slumbering warriors, but some also mention soldiers who constantly roam through the countryside until the Day of Judgement under some holy injunction or geis. One such tale is to be found in County Down and relates to a king who broke his promise to the hosts of the fairy.

King Fintan and the Cursed Wedding Gift

"In ancient times, a king called Fintan ruled the land stretching through the Mournes and beyond. His kingdom reached from the lands around the Narrow Water and far into Armagh. Some say that it even went as far as the borders of Tyrone itself. There is no doubt that he was a mighty warrior for he defeated the Vikings at Warrenpoint and turned back Scottish pirates at Carlingford and they say that he built a line of forts all the way from Newry to the coast of Down to keep raiders and cattle thieves out of his kingdom. It is also said that he was an extremely learned man, very well read, and that he was a great Christian as well, building many churches and abbeys all through the kingdom of Down.

His greatest passion, besides fighting and praying, was hunting and he would often ride all through the Mournes, starting up deer, foxes and hares and chasing them for sport.

Now it came the time for Fintan to be married and I can assure you that there was no shortage of prospective brides, so great was his reputation as a good and wise king. Many kings from Ireland and beyond offered their daughters with the prospect of making an alliance with such a mighty king. At last he settled upon the daughter of one of the kings of Alban in Scotland and arrangements were quickly made for the wedding day.

Marriage arrangements or not, King Fintan was not to be deterred from his hunting and as the sun rose high over the Mournes in the middle of summer he and some of this men rode out to chase down some wolves that had been sorely annoying his people.

They rode for several days, deep into the heart of the mountains, into places that they had never been to before. The land all around became dreary and barren and there were few trees about. Those that reared out of the arid soil were naked and leafless, raising skeletal wooden arms against the failing sun. A chilly wind blew down from the mountains, making King Fintan and his riders shiver from both fear and cold. They decided to turn for home.

But as they were about to do so, they came upon a strange procession wending its way amongst the remains of an ancient and long-dead forest. This was like no procession which they had ever seen before for, although the people before them seemed human enough in form, they were much smaller than ordinary folk and were completely clothed in cowled robes. They walked slowly, like monks, but with a strange and halting step. Thinking them to be some sort of holy men, King Fintan raised his hand in salute and called out a greeting.

The tallest of the small men responded with a greeting of his own, spoken in an ancient tongue which had almost fallen into disuse but which Fintan, with his learning, still understood. The robed figure asked the king to dismount and to join them on their way to a great festival. The king of their own country was getting married and was holding a grand banquet in his palace a little way off. As a visiting monarch himself, Fintan would be the guest of honour and would be most welcome.

Dismounting, Fintan was about to decline the stranger's offer when he saw, peeking out from underneath the long robe, the cloven foot of an animal. Then he knew that these were the last of the *sidhe*, an old goat-footed race that had once dwelt in the high mountains of Ireland before the coming of Saint Patrick and long before Christianity had taken root in the country. A great curiosity overcame him for Fintan was an inquiring scholar and he agreed to go with the strangers and to join in the revels at their king's palace.

So they travelled together through the dreary land until they reached a great cliff-face. There, a mighty cave-mouth yawned before them and the procession passed into it, King Fintan and his retinue following behind. They immediately found themselves in the middle of a great hall carved out of the rock, lit with tapers. Large veins of iron and gold ran through the walls, which had been hung with shields and ancient weaponry, and the roots of trees formed a mighty curtain in front of the stone throne where the goat-footed king sat.

'A thousand welcomes to you, King Fintan of Down', called the small being, moving forward on its seat. 'I am Doel Uldach, King of All the Lands under the Mountains. Come forward and join us in our ceili. Eat and drink of all that we have to offer and join us in our merrymaking, for this is a great day in our country! This is my wedding day!'

King Fintan stepped forward and squinted through the curtain of fine tree-roots. The creature that sat on the throne was small and squat, more like an ape than a human being. Upon his balding head was a crown of great age and beauty and, as Fintan looked more closely, he saw that the other king had indeed the feet of a goat. He was in the presence of the *sidhe* king, monarch of that lightless kingdom to which Saint Patrick had banished the beings of earth and air.

'I greet you in brotherhood, Doel Uldach', he replied most civilly, as any Christian should. 'But I come bearing no gift for this auspicious day.'

Doel Uldach bared his monkey-like teeth.

'There is no need for any such gift', he replied with equal civility, 'for we of the *sidhe* have need of nothing from the sons of the dust. But you are our guests. Come, eat and drink, for soon the dancing is to begin.'

He clapped his taloned hands and tables appeared in the centre of the cavern, groaning with meat and drink in great abundance. The men were about to rush forward and help themselves but King Fintan waved them to wait.

'I must give you something', he persisted, plucking a ruby ring from his finger, 'for I am to be married soon myself and would consider it a great discourtesy if I were not allowed to wish you well.'

Doel Uldach graciously accepted the ring, then waved his hands wide in a grand gesture of welcome.

'Then it is accepted!' he cried. 'Now eat and drink, for we must celebrate my wedding.'

Without further ado, Fintan's men fell upon the tables and began to eat and drink their fill. Fintan, however, was a stout Christian and was hesitant about wilfully eating the food of the pagan *sidhe*. Gradually, however, he succumbed to the spell and fell to eating with his men. All the while, they were serenaded by the sweetest and most ancient airs played by a host of invisible musicians who seemed to be all around them.

In the midst of all the joviality, Fintan and Doel Uldach found themselves sitting beside each other.

'You tell me that you are soon to be married yourself?' asked the *sidhe* king. Fintan nodded.

'I am, to be sure', he replied, 'to the daughter of a Scottish king. I have been a guest at your wedding banquet, you must be a guest at mine!'

He had not meant to issue the invitation to the goat-footed king for he secretly feared the dark magic of the *sidhe*, but the words seemed to tumble from his lips of their own accord. Doel Uldach gave a horrible grimace.

'I thank you, Fintan', he answered very cordially. 'Your kind offer is gratefully accepted!'

There was more music and more revelry. As the day began to break, the festivities came to an end and Fintan and his warriors took their leave of the Lands under the Mountains.

'I shall see you upon the day of your own marriage, Fintan!' called Doel Uldach as they departed. King Fintan only smiled wanly and nodded.

'And you shall be royally entertained', he said, 'for are we not brothers in our kingship?'

Of course, he had no intention of having the *sidhe* king at his own wedding but he could not say so after he and his men had been so regally banquetted. He simply hoped that the strange monarch would never get to hear of the wedding feast and so he would be spared any visitation. Fintan returned to his own kingdom and began to make arrangements for his marriage.

The wedding-day came around and a grand and holy day it was. All the great clerics of Ireland were there and the Primate of Armagh himself, dressed in his sacred robes, came to officiate at the celebration. There was feasting and dancing all day and much drinking and jollification. In the midst of all these festivities, King Fintan's thoughts sometimes turned to Doel Uldach. He prayed that the *sidhe* king had forgotten the hasty invitation and would not come to the wedding.

For a while, it seemed as if his prayers had been answered. Then, just as the party was at its height, a messenger came forward to Fintan with a communication.

'My Lord', he said, bowing low. 'Word has come that there is a procession at the borders of your kingdom. Its leader is a king known as Doel Uldach, who says that he is King of All the Lands under the Mountains. He carries your ring and claims you for an old friend. They beg leave to proceed further and attend your wedding feast as you had invited them to do.'

King Fintan's face grew pale and his hands shook. He looked all around the hosts of prelates and bishops of the holy Christian Church and decided then and there that the pagan *sidhe* should not sit amongst these great and holy men.

'Send word that they are to be turned back', he told the messenger. 'I do not know any Doel Uldach and he is not welcome here at my wedding feast. This procession is not to be admitted! This Doel Uldach is someone that I would rather not meet on such a sacred day as this. These are my orders!'

The messenger nodded and was gone and Fintan returned to his guests. The feast continued and the revelry there became the talk of the countryside for many months afterward.

The wedding passed, days turned into weeks and weeks into months. A year after he had been married, Fintan and his men were hunting once more along the upper reaches of Tollymore Forest. They had pursued a wolf into a great clearing there and, after killing the animal, had paused to rest the horses. As they sat in their saddles and talked, there was a trumpeting sound like that of a mighty horn.

Turning suddenly, Fintan saw a movement between the trees and, as he watched, the cowled forms of the *sidhe* host appeared, moving awkwardly on their goat-feet. The foremost of them threw back his cowl and the king saw that it was Doel Uldach. Fintan had his hand upon his sword and an oath ready upon his lips but the *sidhe* king held up his hand and gave an ape-like smile.

'Stay, good friend!' he said. 'Let there be no excuses for our dismissal from your wedding feast. I am simply come in order to deliver the present which I could not give to you on your wedding day. Once it is given, I will trouble you no more.'

Another of the *sidhe* came forward, carrying in his arms a small animal like a dog or a fox. Fintan gave a surprised exclamation and, at the sound of his voice, the creature started awake and sprang into the arms of the human ruler. The king was taken aback but managed what he thought to be a grateful smile.

'A dog!' he said coldly and disinterestedly. 'What a wonderful present!'

Doel Uldach's smile widened.

'I'm glad you like it for it will be your constant companion throughout the years', he said. 'Until I call that dog from your arms you will never be able to dismount from your horse and will ride forever through these mountains until the Day of Judgement, when the world will be consumed by flame. You and your men will know neither hearth nor home until my curse is lifted. This is your penance for breaking your promise to me!'

And at that, the *sidhe* king and his retinue turned and vanished back among the forest trees. With an angry oath, Fintan made to hurl the dog-like creature to the ground but, try as he might, it would not leave his arms. He attempted to get down from the saddle but found that he could not dismount. In panic, he turned for home.

The legends say that King Fintan and his warriors never returned from the mountains but that they ride continually through the Mournes, seeking an entrance to the kingdom of Doel Uldach so that the goat-footed *sidhe* can call the dog from the king's arms and so let them pass on to their eternal reward. And, on dark and stormy nights when the wind howls across the bogs and the lightning flashes over the mountain peaks across the Mournes, it is still possible to see them as they ride onwards in their desperate and eternal quest."

Prepare to Die

There is a basic urge in all of us to know the time and method of our dying so that we can prepare for it in some way. In both rural and seafaring communities, where the prospect of death is always close, this impetus becomes even more pronounced. It is not surprising, therefore, that such intimations of mortality have found their way into the fabric of rural folklore and that many hearth-side tales incorporate some element of foreboding.

In Ireland, many were the signs of imminent doom, if one cared to look for them. A bird flying into the house and refusing to leave, for example, was a sure sign that death was following close behind. Similarly, a candle inexplicably going out signalled a death in the family within the year. A dead bird found on the window-sill first thing in the morning, or three inexplicable raps upon the window or door late at night, foretold either the misfortune or death of a loved one.

But the most feared of all death warnings was the coshtabower or coach-a-bower – the death coach – which travelled invisibly through the Irish countryside collecting souls as it went. Like the banshee it sometimes followed certain families, arriving at the time of death to carry loved-ones away to whatever reward awaited them. This story, collected from an old woman living high in the Sperrin mountains of County Tyrone, tells of two encounters with this phantom.

The Coach-a-bower

"This happened long ago when I was only a slip of a girl, living on the edge of the Sperrins. We lived in a very lonely place, beside a road which ran through the mountains and down into Pomeroy, twisting and turning like an eel as it did so. I must have been about twelve or thirteen when all this first took place. There was a turf-stack a little ways down the road and, every night, one of us young ones had to go down to it and get some peats for the fire. This night, at the very edge of winter, it was my turn to go and so I set off to bring home a bag of it.

It was a clear and frosty night with the moon as big as a shilling and twice as bright and I wasn't afraid of anything in those days. The turf had been brought out of the bog about a week before, so it was very dry, but it was also very heavy. That didn't bother me much for I was big and strong for a girl. I heaved the bag up onto my shoulders and turned for home, walking a bit slow on account of the weight.

Well, I had only taken a couple of steps towards our house when I heard the sound of wheels on the road behind me. It was louder than you would have heard from a pony and trap and it was coming up on me very quick. I thought it might be one of our neighbours in a hurry, so I turned to see who it was and what was wrong. The road lay behind me, twisting and curling across the hills and, because of the moonlight, I could see along its length for miles. There wasn't a thing on it. I looked again to make sure that I hadn't been mistaken but it was still empty as you please. Yet all the time I could hear the sound of wheels drawing closer.

I thought that it might be a cart or carriage some distance away and that the frosty air was making the sound travel, so I put down the turf-sack and waited to see if anything would come into view. Still I saw nothing and the sound drew closer and closer but the divil-a-thing did I see, although I looked and looked. Then, suddenly, it was right up beside me and I was pushed tight up against the ditch as if something was trying to get past me. And still there was nothing to be seen, nothing at all. There was just the fields, white with frost, and the empty road all around me. The best way that I can describe it was that it was like trying to push into a strong wind and the whole night was filled with its sound.

And then it was gone by me and away down the road before me. I heard the sound of its wheels getting further and further from me and still there was nothing to be seen, even though the moonlight was as clear as day.

Well, you wouldn't believe the speed that I made home. I left the bag of turf standing in the middle of the road and ran for dear life. I'd have outstripped the best runner in the district, so I would, just to get to my own front door and shut it tight after me. I told all in the house what I'd heard but nobody would believe me and my father made me go back for the bag of turf. They all made such fun of me that I eventually began to believe that the experience had been nothing more than my own imagination.

Anyway, with other things going on, I'd all but forgotten about the whole affair when, some time after, I was talking to an old woman, Ellen Bradley, who used to come about our house. She was greatly regarded as a wise woman in the locality and was always telling stories about the fairies and of the ghosts who wandered across the mountains. I told her about the noise that I'd heard on the road. At the very mention of it, she started up and crossed herself.

'God between us and harm!' says she. 'It's not right that such a young person should hear these things! That was the coshta-bower – the death coach – that you surely heard. There is misery for some poor crathur somewhere in this locality in its passing.'

She told me that the coshta-bower, or the coach-a-bower as it is sometimes called, carried death into a neighbourhood. It was a death warning like a banshee, she said, but it was never seen at all. The sound of its wheels were sometimes heard going past upon the road outside on frosty nights and if they stopped by a door then you knew that death would visit that house. Well, as you might guess, this greatly troubled me for a time and I watched anxiously to see if anyone in our district would die.

There was a man who lived further along the road, just below us, who was very fond of the drink. They said that he was very bad to his wife and I had often seen him passing by our house, coming from some pub or other, in a great state of intoxication. One evening, about two months after I had heard the coshta-bower, he came past our door, more drunk than usual, and passed on down the road towards his own house. As he was going past our turf-stack, didn't the drink trip him up and he fell heavily at the very place that I had heard the sound. He cut his leg badly but, being a strong enough man and well full of the drink, he never gave it much attention. It swelled up with blood poisoning a couple of days after and they had to rush him to the hospital in Omagh where I heard that he died in spite of everything that the doctors could do for him. That was why the coshta-bower had been on our road, leaving death and grief in its wake.

What I heard at that time was a death-warning sure enough and it was a long, long time before anybody could get me to go back to the turf-stack after that!

I only heard the coach-a-bower one other time, about three or four years after the experience at the turf-stack. This was when my sister Annie was taken very ill with the pneumonia and had to be kept in her bed. I must have been in my sixteenth year at the time.

This happened on a cold winter's evening, when my mother had gone down to see her sister who was married and lived in Pomeroy. My father was still out at work and I was in the house on my own, looking after Annie and waiting for my mother's return. While I was waiting, a neighbour of ours, Maggie Donnelly, called to see how Annie was and I encouraged her to stay for a while. I knew that my mother was in very low spirits about Annie and that she would enjoy Maggie's crack when she returned. Maggie readily agreed and I made some tea for the both of us and, in truth, the stories which she told greatly lifted my own spirits.

As we sat talking by the fire, I heard a sound far away on the Pomeroy road, like a horse and trap, approaching our house very quickly. It was a sound like the 'clop-clop' of horses' hooves on the frosty road, hurrying onward through the gathering dark to get home. It drew closer and closer then, all of a sudden, it seemed to slow down. I thought that it might be one of my uncles giving Mother a lift home from her sister's place or some neighbour coming to see how Annie was.

'There's Mother now', says I, getting up to go to the door. And sure enough, the sound stopped when it drew level with our house. I went to the window to look out before I opened the door for I wanted to see who had left her home. There was nothing at all to be seen on the road outside. Then I thought back to the night by the turf-stack and the coshta-bower that had pushed past me those three or four years before. Suddenly, I heard three low but very clear raps. I don't know if they came from the window or the door but I can vouch that I heard them distinctly. They were like the noise of a stick hitting the bottom of an empty wooden bucket – sort of hollow-sounding and echoing and shivery. It wasn't a good sound to hear at all.

I know that Maggie heard them too for she jumped up with a start and looked around her, as if trying to see where they had come from. Then, without warning, the coach wheels started on the road outside again, heading away up into the mountains. The sound grew fainter and fainter until it died away altogether and I heard it no more. Maggie became very pale and crossed herself.

'Come away from the window, Mary!' says she, very sternly. 'That was the coach-a-bower come for your sister's soul. Don't look out for you don't know what you might see! Annie is not long for this world at all!'

Soon after, my mother came home and we told her what had happened. I don't know whether she believed us or not for she was a very level-headed woman. There were always old stories in the countryside about three knocks on the window preceding a death, but she had never paid them any heed. She went in to look at Annie, who was sleeping soundly. We thought that she seemed to be improving a little bit. After Maggie had left and my father had come home, we all went to our beds and I tried to put the strange experience to the back of my mind.

Later that night, however, Annie's fever got worse and she took a turn. A doctor was sent for but it was morning before he could get to our house and my sister was already dead. The death coach had come for her soul all right!

I heard afterwards that a number of other people in our locality had heard the coach-a-bower that same night. It had passed by their houses but all of them were afraid to look out.

Many had guessed that it was coming to our house. Sometime after, I was speaking to people in our neighbourhood and they said that they had heard it on another occasion as well. When an old man called Barnett died some years ago, away across the mountains, everybody in the district heard the death coach going past their doors as it went for his soul.

They say that it is the devil himself who drives it and that the horses that pull it are all headless but that no mortal eye can see it as it goes past. Three raps on the window are a sure sign that death is in a house but if the coach only stops at a door then it is a signal that there will be a lasting sickness in that place. That was what I heard anyway.

There are those, too, who will tell you nowadays that these are only old stories told by superstitious people and that any sound that you might hear on the road is only the smugglers running their poteen down to Pomeroy from stills away up in the mountains. They say that it is the smugglers themselves that put these stories about to keep people from seeing them as they pass. But I'm an old woman now and I've no cause to lie. I know what I heard all those years ago and I know the way that it was."

Tales of the coach-a-bower were once common all through the Sperrins, in County Down, County Monaghan and in Dublin itself. At one time they were as prolific as stories about the banshee. The original Irish name, coiste bodhar, *literally means deaf coach, although no explanation is offered for this particular name.*

Creaking carts and coaches, however, were not the only foretellers of doom, for the rolling and mysterious sea also contains several prognostications of death. The changing coast-

line of Ireland has given rise to many stories concerning death-warnings, often featuring some of the coastal towns and villages which have slipped into the ocean over the course of time. Many are said to still lie far beneath the waves, and sometimes the sun can be seen glinting on their sunken rooves below the water. It is not a good omen to see such sights, as the following old and persisting story from West Clare warns.

The Bells of the Drowned Town

"They say that between the Cliffs of Moher and the Ballard Cliffs further south, there used to be a great stretch of farming land, fairly covered with houses and towns. The biggest of all these was Kilstaveen on the west Clare coast at which there was a large and important monastery. But even though it was a holy place, there was still great wickedness in that town. The weekly market which was held there, for instance, was full of rogues and thieves who would rob an honest trader and there was always great drunkenness about its streets and badness in its houses. Whilst they were aware of all the roguery that was going on, the monks in the town, to their shame, did nothing at all to stop it, nor did they even say a word against it.

Then, some time in the past, there was a great earthquake which shook the entire coast of Ireland, sending much land sliding into the sea. And the shock split the ground between Moher and Ballard and the land between collapsed into the water, together with the town of Kilstaveen and its monastery. The earthquake struck late at night and so the people there were all drowned as they slept in their beds. No one was spared. Many said it was God's judgement on the unholy town and its inhabitants.

I heard the old people say that Kilstaveen is still there beneath the water, in a bay to the south of Lahinch and that, on a clear and sunny day when the sea is still, you can sometimes glimpse the walls of a house or the spire of the monastery directly below the surface of the ocean. But to see it is an evil sign which betokens disaster for the seer, for Kilstaveen is a haunted place where the ghosts of those that died there that night still dwell. I can tell you that many fishermen along the Clare shoreline still live in dread to this day of seeing the ruined walls or the weed-covered bell-tower of that lost place. And sometimes, at night, the monastery bell can yet be heard ringing out across the waves. To hear that is a sure sign that death is not far away.

You ask me how I know of these things? Well, when I was a lad of about 14 years of age, I sailed on a fine summer's day on a fishing-boat out of Doonbeg up towards Galway Bay. The air was very still and the sea as clear and as untroubled as polished glass. We had sailed near some rocky shoals where there was supposed to be a big draught of fish and had just let down our nets when, out across the water, I thought that I heard a faint sound, like the steady tolling of a bell, very far away. I cocked my ears and strained to listen but the sound didn't come again. Almost at once, from the stern of the boat, came the cry:

'Kilstaveen! Kilstaveen! Oh God, protect us!'

We all turned to see what was going on. One of the men there was staring into the sunlit depths of the sea and was pointing with a trembling finger at something far below its surface. Several of us younger crewmen ran forward to see what was happening although the older men, who knew the story, stayed back and turned their heads away, fearful of what they might see. We looked but saw nothing only the sun glinting on the waves. The man, however, kept pointing.

'Can you not see it?' he shouted wildly. 'Look, there are the walls of the houses and there is the spire of a church. Oh God, it has to be Kilstaveen!'

In an instant, a freak wave arose from nowhere and swept over the stern of the boat, carrying away the trembling man with it but leaving the rest of us untouched. He vanished beneath the water and didn't rise again. The wave passed as soon as it had arisen and the sea was as calm and still as it had been before. But the man was gone all right and although we searched for hours, not a trace of him did we find. He had been taken to dwell with the undersea ghosts that live in Kilstaveen.

We sailed back to Doonbeg in sorrowing silence and it was there that I heard the story of the sunken town and its evil curse. Several fishermen from the area had thought they had seen something beneath the waves and all of them had died shortly after. Sometimes whole boat-crews had been lost. I spoke about the bell-like sound that I had heard and the old men nodded and said that it was a death-sign sure enough. Other crews had also heard it and their boats had been surrounded by strange and inexplicable fogs. When these lifted some of the men were gone, perhaps fallen into the ocean or carried off by creatures from the waters. Ghostly hands tolled the monastery bell to announce the arrival of a new soul to their dead and watery world. The very thought of it sent a shiver all through me. I had heard the bell-note sure enough and yet nothing has befallen me to this day, and I pray God that it never will.

That's a true story. I always stayed away from that particular area after that but, at certain times, I have thought that I heard the note of a bell, tolling away across the ocean, and always there has been a tragedy shortly afterwards. Sometimes, if they think that they hear that bell-note, Clare fishermen will not even put to sea, no matter how calm the weather, for they know that if they do, they may never return home again. That is the curse of Kilstaveen, the drowned town."

It is easy to dismiss this story as irrational nonsense. Fishermen and mariners, after all, are said to be amongst the most superstitious of men and the glimpse of any sunken wall might be enough to startle them and give rise to such stories as that about Kilstaveen. And yet, who knows, for the sea is often as mysterious as it is dangerous and many strange things come and go in its depths.

Sometimes death warnings take a more human form. The banshee is well-known across Ireland in the form of a small, wizened woman, keening in the moonlight. A tale from County Monaghan refers to yet another seemingly human warning which portends doom and death.

The Graveyard Bride

"Away in the County Monaghan, in the Barony of Truagh, there is an old churchyard, now badly overgrown and weed-choked, that was once used by a number of important families in the area. It is widely known as Eringle Truagh and, although the church which it served has long gone to ruin and is no longer standing, the churchyard was still used for burials into this present century. It is said that the church was dismantled in 1835 and now nothing remains but two ivy-covered towers rising into the evening sky.

It is not a good place to be for the lowering skies cast it into a sort of darkness, especially coming into the winter time, and the wind moans eerily amongst the stunted trees which rise up like broken fingers amongst the grass-swathed headstones. Old legends in the countryside round about state that it is haunted by a very peculiar spirit which warns of impending death. The apparition is said to take two distinctive forms. If the person who sees it is a man, then it will take the shape of a beautiful young girl; if the viewer is a girl, then it appears as a handsome man. Always it is seen within the walls of the churchyard; always late in the evening; always it approaches someone who has lingered over-long after a funeral; and always it is seen by someone whose doom approaches.

In the autumn of 1895, a young man called John Torney was wandering through the churchyard examining the headstones and taking in the general atmosphere of the old place. He had been attending a burial there and had lingered behind to look at the grave markers, some of which were very old. Although his family was originally Irish, John Torney himself did not come from Ireland but had travelled from the North of England to attend the funeral and had become enamoured of the rolling landscape of his forebears in County Monaghan. Now he was having one last walk around the churchyard before going home.

As he walked, he became aware of someone else. Away across the clumps of long grass and slanting funeral stones, a woman was passing quickly between the graves, pausing only to examine some faded inscriptions here and there. As Torney looked at her, he was struck by how young she seemed to be and also by how very beautiful she was. Her hair was long and dark and hung loosely about her shoulders in the fashion of Irish women, her narrow face was pale but strikingly attractive, and yet it seemed to be drawn in deepest despair. She was dressed in a long and flowing, white filmy gown which seemed, to Torney, to bear an uncanny resemblance to an old-style wedding dress. She moved with a swift, almost jerky motion, hurrying here and there, bending down to read some eroded script and then passing on to another headstone.

It was now growing dark and the air had become very chilly. Still the strange girl showed no sign of leaving. Indeed, as gloom descended on that ancient churchyard, she appeared to become more and more agitated, flitting ever more quickly amongst the headstones.

Intrigued by her odd behaviour, Torney approached her.

'Can I help you?' he asked. 'Are you looking for something?' She shook her head and explained that she had come to the churchyard to wait for a man (Torney assumed him to be her lover) but, now that the light was failing, she was frightened that he wouldn't turn up. She asked the young man to wait with her for a time to see if the other would show up and, rather reluctantly, John Torney agreed to do so. Sitting down on a flat tombstone, they waited, talking as they did so. The girl asked many questions about Torney – where he came from, what he did, why he was in Ireland, how long he was staying – but ventured no information about herself, and when he tried to ask her, she deftly changed the subject.

At length it became quite dark and it was now apparent that the girl's assignation would not take place. However, Torney had surprisingly enjoyed the conversation with his strange partner and, although he was returning to England the following day, he asked the girl her name once more so that he might write to her. She shook her head.

'I will not give you my name now', she answered, 'but let us meet again, on this spot, one year from this evening and you will know everything about me.' And, before he could answer her, she had leapt up and was gone amongst the headstones, weaving her way between them. He tried to look after her and see where she went but a bird called somewhere close by and the sound made him involuntarily turn his head for a second. When he turned back, he was alone in the churchyard.

John Torney went back to his lodgings, turning over the strange incident in his mind. He could make no sense of it at all. The next morning, over breakfast, he mentioned it to his host, hoping that the other might shed some light as to who the strange girl might be and where he might find her. Imagine his surprise when the man turned quite pale and crossed himself.

'In the name of God!' he exclaimed. 'That was no human woman that you met with. That was the Churchyard Bride that haunts Eringle Truagh! That was a warning that you are not long for this world!' And with a tremble in his voice he proceeded to tell John Torney the legend of the graveyard spectre.

'There are many stories about this phantom. Some say that it is that of a young bride who was jilted on her wedding day by an unscrupulous suitor. Others say that it was a bridegroom who took his life after his promised bride had deserted him. Whatever it is, it haunts the old churchyard around the dark time of the year. Only those who are about to die can see it. It often engages them in pleasant conversation, but in the end it will extract a promise to meet them again in Eringle Truagh within one year. That will be the date of their death! The phantom has never been wrong yet but it has been a long time since anyone in this locality has actually seen it. Go and seek out a priest and have him pray for your soul.'

His host's words shocked Torney for, although he was not a superstitious man, they had a ring of truth about them. A shiver passed through him, almost as if a cold finger had run along the length of his spine. He made further enquiries in the surrounding countryside and was told the same story, which gave him no grain of comfort. He was now of the opinion that he was a marked man and that not even the offices of the Church could spare him from whatever fate awaited him.

The next day, John Torney returned to England but the spectral warning continued to haunt him even there. He sank into a deep melancholy and began to shun the company of his former friends, becoming something of a recluse. He became increasingly obsessed until he thought of nothing else, falling deeper and deeper into gloom, despair and eventually sickness.

Acquaintances remarked how pale and gaunt he had become, that the flesh seemed to fall away from his bones as though he was suffering from some fatal fever. Many advised him to seek out medical help. Torney, however, ignored them and continued to brood on the warning.

A year had all but passed when he made a resolution. The spectre had suggested that they meet in the churchyard of Eringle Truagh a year after their first encounter. He would return there to find her waiting for him and would plead with her to lift the curse which hung like a pall over his whole being. To this end, he set out again for Ireland and County Monaghan, hopeful that his pleadings would help avert his fate.

The ancient churchyard was very much as he remembered it. It was late in the year and the lowering clouds hung darkly above the tumbled and overgrown headstones. Carefully making his way among the weathered grave-markers, John Torney looked around for the spectre but saw nothing. He was on the point of leaving the place when, from the corner of his eye, he glimpsed a movement away across the churchyard. It was the spectre, coming from among the tombs towards him. He fell back but a strange power pulled him forward to meet her. She threw her arms wide and he went to her.

They found the body of John Torney seated on a flat gravestone on the edge of the graveyard of Eringle Truagh. He was quite dead. As he was a young man, an inquest was held but it concluded that he had died of a heart attack. Many of his friends had attested that he had not been in good health of late, and how could the law take account of a ghost or its death warning?

It is said that the spectre still haunts the old churchyard and its legend is well known. The writer, William Carleton, wrote a ballad about it called 'Sir Turlough and the Churchyard Bride', and it has been mentioned in many old stories from the area. It has not been seen recently, possibly because no young person would wander alone in an old overgrown graveyard in these times. But when the winter sky is low over the gravestones, something white – like a bride's gown – can sometimes still be seen darting amongst the stunted bushes deep in the ancient cemetery. At least that is what they say in the countryside around the churchyard of Eringle Truagh, away in the County Monaghan."

Brides from the Sea

Legends of mermaids and sea creatures have always been common around the Irish coast. From North Antrim to Kerry they have woven themselves into the tapestry of Irish myth. It would be wrong to assume that Irish mermaids correspond exactly to their traditional and well-known English counterparts – half-woman, half-fish. Celtic merfolk, rather, display more of the attributes of the seal than they do of any fish. This belief probably has its origins in the abundance of seals around Gaelic shores.

Mermaids in Ireland were often known as "silkies" (a name by which they are also known in Scotland) and they travelled through the water wrapped in sealskin cloaks. Shedding these cloaks, they came ashore in human form to dance and play along the shoreline and amongst the rocks. If a mortal were to find one of these cloaks and take it away and hide it, the mermaid could not return to the sea and would be forced to do the bidding of the human. In many cases this entailed marriage, for mermaids in their human form were believed to be very beautiful. Many ancient Irish families – the O'Flahertys and the O'Sullivans of Kerry, and the MacNamaras from Clare, for example – claim they can trace their descendency from unions between mermaids and humans.

Mermaids could take other shapes and sometimes wandered about the seashore in the guise of small, hornless cattle (fairy cows) or seabirds. But it was mostly in the guise of the seal that the silkies were seen. The creatures were often to be spotted basking among the coastal rocks, sometimes speaking to the passer-by in a human (Gaelic) tongue. Of all the fairy kind, it was the merfolk who actively sought out human company and established relationships with mortal families. One such was with the Cantillon family of County Kerry.

The Last Funeral of the Cantillons

"You will have heard of the Cantillons, I'm sure, for they were an important family in Kerry. You will probably know too that their ancient burial place was on an island, close to the shore, in Ballyheigue Bay. At some time in the past, this island may have been part of the mainland but gradually the sea seems to have overwhelmed it, enveloping part of it beneath the waves. There was an old church on it, all of it in ruins, and this seems to have been swallowed up by the sea, along with the old cemetery. On a clear and sunny day, the Kerry fishermen claimed that they could see its walls, overgrown with seaweed, together with ancient tombs, far beneath them as they sailed along the coast.

You may also have heard of a curious custom amongst the Cantillons regarding their burial. So attached were they to their traditional burying-place that they refused to be buried anywhere else, even though the churchyard now lay far beneath the sea. Consequently, when any family member died their coffined corpse was carried at evening to the seashore, where it was left on Ballyheigue Strand within reach of the tide. After the customary religious observances had been carried out, the funeral party retired as night was about to fall, without a backward glance. In the morning the coffin was gone, conveyed away, it was believed, by the sea-folk to the burying ground beneath the sea under the terms of an ancient agreement. This had been the way of it for centuries.

There was one man who had married into the family who didn't believe in that old tradition. His name was Connor Crowe and he was a Clare man who had married one of the Cantillon girls. Connor was a hard-headed man and not given to any kind of superstition and so he refused to give the burial-custom any sort of credence.

'The tide washes the body out to sea where it is lost among the currents', he proclaimed scoffingly. 'Doubtless if you were to search around the shores elsewhere, you'd find coffins and bodies washed up. So much for ancient tradition!' The others in the family, however, shook their heads and kept to their custom.

On the death of Florence Cantillon, Connor Crowe decided to prove them all wrong. Flory Cantillon was a well-known and popular man and his funeral attracted country people from Tarbert to Dingle and beyond and was a grand and stately occasion. On hearing about the old man's death, Connor Crowe set out to the Cantillon's church at Ardfert where the service was being conducted before the walk to Ballyheigue strand. Once the service was finished and the corpse had been properly keened in the Irish fashion, a small procession of mourners walked down to the strand to leave the coffin within reach of the tide. Amongst them was Connor Crowe, who went under the guise of paying his last respects to the old man. In truth, he was preparing to test the legend.

As custom dictated, the coffin was left on the sand, just above the line of the tide, and the requisite prayers were said for the dead. Then the funeral party departed for Ardfert. Connor, however, waited behind to see what happened. He hid himself amongst several large stones, high above the strand, where he could clearly see the coffin on the sand.

The moon was big and bright and flooded the beach with a light which lit up the shore as clear as day. Fortifying himself with some whiskey from a bottle which he had brought with him, Connor waited and watched. Nothing happened, and the coffin lay untouched upon the strand below. The hours crawled by with nothing stirring. Around two o'clock, he was on the point of calling it a night and following the others back to Ardfert when he became aware of a strange sound – like the noise of Irish keening – coming from the sea. He squinted in the direction of the beach. The black coffin still lay there, just above the line of the tide. The keen came closer and he realised that it was of such an exquisite sweetness that no mortal tongue could have uttered it. It seemed to rise and fall with the swell of the sea, drawing closer and closer all the while.

Then, rising out of the incoming tide, he saw four strange figures, walking through the water towards the sandy shore. They seemed cowled and robed like monks and appeared to be strangely stooped and bowed. They moved awkwardly, sidling through the surf like giant crabs, their long clothes trailing strands of seaweed behind them. Although he strained to glimpse their faces in the moonlight, Connor saw nothing, for their heads were almost completely enveloped by the great hoods that they wore.

The keen came to an end and the creatures gathered around the coffin on the strand. With quick, awkward movements, they stooped over it and began to push it towards the rolling waves, muttering amongst themselves as they did so. Connor Crowe felt a thrill of fear pass through his body for he knew that these creatures were not human. Yet he was also seized with a great curiosity to find out who or what they were. He leaned forward on his high perch, straining to hear what was being said.

'How many more centuries will we be condemned to carry out this task?' asked one in clear but hollow tones. 'For long aeons we have been bound by our promise to carry the mortal dead to their final resting place in the sunken church and I grow weary of it.' Another inclined its hooded head as if in a nod.

'This is what comes from marrying amongst mortal kind', answered another as it pushed the coffin a little further out.

The waves reached for it hungrily.

'The promise was made in a time long past when our people freely consorted with those who lived on the land. The daughter of one of our ancient kings married with a forebear of one of the Cantillons and was buried in that now-ruined place upon their funeral island. The island itself was overwhelmed by the sea and since that time we have been compelled to convey the Cantillon dead to those ancient tombs beneath the waves. There will be no respite from this onerous task until the Day of Judgement.'

A third held up its hand, and Connor Crowe trembled because he saw that it had only three long and clawed fingers.

'Wait!' it boomed. 'You are mistaken. A time will come when we shall be freed from our old obligation:

When mortal eye our work shall spy,
And human ear our dirge shall hear.

It is then that our burial of the Cantillon dead shall be at an end and we can remain forever in the sea. This was part of that ancient agreement.'

'When will that be?' asked the fourth in its sepulchral voice, but the others only shook their heads and contineued to push the coffin further out into the ocean. A wave caught it and bore it away and the creatures prepared to follow. Connor Crowe, still perched on the rocks above, leaned forward to hear if anything further was to be said but the whiskey had made him careless and he upset a couple of stones in front of him, sending them tumbling down the slope onto the beach. At that sound, one of the creatures turned its head and Connor had the briefest glimpse of a hideous, green-scaled face with long, dagger-like teeth. The unearthly thing raised a hand and pointed at him as he stood, transfixed with fear.

'Behold!' it cried. 'A mortal spies upon us in our work! The time has come! A mortal eye has gazed upon the children of the foam and a mortal ear has heard their plaintive voices. The cycle is complete. No longer are the sons of the sea condemned to bury the spawn of the dust. Farewell to the Cantillons!'

And with that they turned and moved jerkily out into the rolling swell, slowly following the coffin as it sank beneath the surface of the rolling sea. Connor watched them until they disappeared from sight over the submerged churchyard and the ocean was empty. Then, with a shiver, he turned and fled homeward to Ardfert.

From that day on, none of the Cantillon dead has ever been left on Ballyheigue strand. All are conveyed to a family burying-ground in Ardfert. The ancient church still lies beneath the waves of the Atlantic and no doubt strange creatures still pass to and fro about its ruins, but the age-old agreement between humans and the sea-people is now and forever at an end."

We tend to think of mermaids as shy, beautiful creatures who would harm no-one, whereas many legends portray them as evil creatures whose sole intent is to lure mortals into the waves and drown them. It was a common belief, therefore, that no-one should fall asleep on the seashore unless it was within the sound of church bells. The belief may, of course, stem from actual incidents where sleeping persons were borne away and drowned by an incoming tide but the idea persisted. Church bells were said to drive the evil beings away since no mermaid could withstand the holy sound. The following story is from Athlone.

The Soldier's Bonnet

"There are those who will tell you that mermaids are gentle creatures with no harm about them. This is not the way of it at all. Mermaids are dark and evil beings, the spawn of the devil himself, and no Christian man, if he values his soul, should have anything to do with them.

There is an island in the Shannon, near Athlone, where a mermaid sits on the rocks combing her hair and admiring herself in a small, silver hand-mirror. To see her sitting there is an evil thing for it either foretells some terrible disaster or means that a crime is being committed somewhere near at hand; for she is an evil spirit and never appears except to announce ill-luck, in which she takes an unholy delight.

One day, a young fisherman was casting his nets along the river when he was drawn towards this particular island by a strong and mysterious current. Although he struggled with the tiller of his boat, he could not prevent it from being pulled onto the rocks and dashed to pieces. He fell down through the foaming waters – down, down, until he felt that his lungs would burst. The darkness of the river took him and he lost consciousness.

He did not die but woke to find himself lying on the side of a beautiful hill in a strange country that he had never seen before.

Low and rolling hills, covered in strange bell-like flowers, stretched away on either side of him and a mellow, golden haze seemed to permeate everything around him. At first he thought that he might be in paradise itself but then it came to him that he was not dead but in some mysterious land, far below the river. There was a faint singing in the air, like the single clear note of a bell or the sound of a sweet but inhuman voice singing in a persistent tone. He followed the sound across the country and before long came upon a mermaid sitting in a garlanded bower at the edge of a small, still pool. She was combing her hair and looking into her hand-mirror with great attention. The fisherman approached her cautiously for he knew that this was an enchanted place. At his approach, the mermaid lay down her mirror and greeted him with the most dazzling of smiles.

'Welcome, mortal', she said pleasantly. 'I have been waiting for you to come to me. It was I who drew your boat across the waters far above and it was I who dashed it against the rocks there. Please do not think badly of me for I only did it so that I might have some company in my lonely world here in the depths. I only did it out of despair at my empty life.'

She spoke so sweetly and so pleadingly that the fisherman could not help but feel sorry for her. That is the way of it with the water-people; they can enchant and beguile you with their honeyed words and with the tone of their voice. Her captive could not see her for the evil sprite she was. He sat down with her in the bower whilst she sang to him in a pure, clear voice and soon he had all but forgotten his family and friends and the world above the waves.

'Stay with me forever, mortal', the mermaid pleaded. 'See, I will give you a goblet of wine and when you drink this, you will forget your own world entirely.' And so saying, she stretched forth a golden goblet which was fairly brimming with what appeared to be the finest red wine. The fisherman accepted it, raised it to his lips and was about to drink when he saw to his horror that what she had offered him was, in fact, blood. He thrust it away from him in disgust. The mermaid, however, appeared not at all worried.

'You surely must be hungry', she said in the same silky tone. 'Let me offer you something to eat.' And, drawing back into the bower, she opened a small cupboard, beckoning him to come forward. He peered into her small store and saw, to his intense terror, that she had the body of a drowned soldier, still wearing his army greatcoat, stored there. The corpse looked back at him with unseeing eyes and, as he looked, the fisherman saw that its throat had been cut. With a loud cry he fell backwards, making the sign of the cross, and darkness overwhelmed him.

He soon came to, however, and found himself on the rocks in the Shannon amid the wreck of his boat. There he lay until his friends, who had been searching for him, found him and brought him home.

The unfortunate man's story does not end there, for tucked into his belt was the cap of the dead soldier and it was stained with blood. The police wanted to know how he had come by it and they arrested him on suspicion of murder. For a day and a night he lay languishing in jail with no-one to believe his story. He was sent for trial and might have been hanged had not several witnesses come forward to testify on his behalf.

The cap belonged to a soldier, they said, who had been a deserter from Athlone Barracks and, on being pursued, had cut his own throat and had flung himself over a bridge and into the Shannon. This was the very corpse that the fisherman had seen in that bower in the country far beneath the water, for it is well known that such suicides often become the property of mermaids and other dark things. The fisherman was released and went straightaway to a priest to make confession and receive an exorcism. Thereafter, the wicked siren of the rocks troubled him no more, although she continues to be seen until this very day, sitting in the midst of the Shannon and gloating over every misfortune that befalls mankind. If you pass by the river shore late of an evening, you may see her yet. Only the sign of the Holy Cross will protect you against the work of such things. God between us and all harm!"

Several mermaids have married mortals, though such marriages are never easy. Often the mermaid is tricked into marrying the man and, although she is a good wife to him, she will yearn to return to the sea and will eventually do so. She will leave husband and family behind her for she is, in the first instance, a creature of the ocean. The following tale demonstrates tensions which can exist in unions between humans and merfolk. It is a variation of an old story from North Antrim, although the story itself is told all over Ireland.

The Three Blows

"I well remember my grandmother telling this story as a warning that you should never marry a mermaid.

There was a man named Tom Harte who lived at the foot of the Glens where the land runs into the sea. Like many around him, he was a fisherman by trade and was often to be seen fishing from the rocks on the rocky coast above the village of Glenarm.

One morning, he arrived in his customary spot to find a

mysterious woman sitting there. She was dressed in a long, green cloak and her dark hair hung in ringlets about her beautiful face. Her lips seemed exceptionally red and her eyes were as green and cold as the ocean itself. She engaged Tom Harte in conversation whilst he went about setting his lines but he was wary of answering her for he feared that she might be one of the sea people. Her manner, however, was quite pleasant and, gradually, she began to win him round.

The next day he came to the same spot and she was there, waiting for him again. He asked her questions about herself but she did not answer, or evaded them in some way, and he became more and more convinced that she was some being from the sea come to seek out a mortal mate. This is often the custom with the sea people for they are greatly interested in mortals and to have a human partner is a great honour amongst them. All the same, the prospect now did not seem to matter to him and it did not alarm him as much as it had before. He chatted to her quite freely and she laughed and joked with him. Her laughter was as clear as a ship's bell far out at sea on a foggy night, and Tom Harte found it extremely pleasant.

Each day from then onwards, when he went down to the rocks below the village to set his lines, he found the woman waiting for him and they would talk freely. As time went on, he found himself being drawn to her and, as he lay alone in his bed of a night, he began to think how grand it would be if she were lying there beside him. His thoughts were now turning towards marriage. He had been warned, of course, that a union between humans and the sea people was not a good thing but he was besotted with the strange woman and put such reservations to the back of his mind.

One day at the heels of the summer, as they sat together on the rocks, he asked her to marry him. The woman sat for a long time looking out across the rolling sea before she answered. When she did, it was with a certain coldness in her voice that she spoke, a coldness that matched the chill in her green eyes.

'I will marry you, Tom Harte, if that is your wish', she answered, 'and I will bear you a fine child. But our marriage will not be an easy one for I will be a demanding wife.'

Tom, nevertheless, was not to be turned. He promised, on the grave of his dead mother, that he would be the best husband to her in the whole of north Antrim, no, in the whole of Ireland itself! The woman considered further.

'If I come to you as your wife, I will not come empty-handed, for my family is a very old one and has amassed a great fortune. I am used to the best and can take my pick of many suitors. Nevertheless, I am minded to take you for my husband if you will be good to me. You must give me what I ask, even though you can ill afford it', she went on, 'and you must be patient and kind to me and you must never strike me for any reason.'

Tom protested at the very thought of it but the sea-woman held up her hand. 'If you strike me three times, for any reason at all, then I will return from whence I came and you will see me no more. If you agree to all these conditions, then I will become your wife.'

Despite the conditions that she had heaped upon the union, Tom Harte readily agreed to them. Maybe his head was turned with her beauty or maybe she had placed some sort of enchantment upon him, for that is the way of the sea-folk. In any case, he wanted her more than anything.

So it was that the sea-woman became Tom Harte's wife. They were not wedded in a church, as far as I am aware, but rather in the old Irish style of a country marriage (marriage by common consent and without the benefit of clergy) and, in all the time that she lived amongst mortals, the woman never entered a church or place of worship. This was because she was one of the sea people who shun all things that men find holy.

As she had promised, she did not come to the marriage empty-handed for she brought a chestful of ancient golden coins that had most probably been sunk with some long-drowned ship. Together with this, she also brought a gold plate and some silver ornaments.

Tom could use some of the coins from the chest but the plate and the ornaments were hers and she always kept them by her. The fisherman was so taken with his new wife that he was content to take whatever she doled out to him and, although he now appeared to have plenty of money about him, he didn't give up the fishing.

Many of the old people shook their heads and prophesied that no good would come of a marriage between a mortal and a woman from the sea. One old woman who lived away up in Glenshesk, and who was regarded as a wise-woman in the countryside round about, gave him a stark and bitter warning:

'It is not given that the children of Adam should marry with the creatures of the ocean', she said. 'No good will come of it. Mark my words, tears will flow before it is all ended and those tears will be as salt as the sea itself.'

Tom Harte, however, ignored the prophesy, so enamoured by his new bride was he, and they moved into a small cottage by the seashore.

Time passed. Months drifted into years and the fisherman and his wife seemed happy enough. There were those, of course, who said that the woman was cruel and demanding to her husband but, if that was indeed the case, Tom made no outward show of it. The money which his wife had brought with her certainly made life a little easier for him and he didn't have to work quite so hard. He was not overly rich but he was not poor either. Indeed, he became something of a gentleman in the locality, consorting with several of the landowners round about and sometimes even being invited to their parties and balls.

One night, when he was planning to attend a gathering given by one of the country squires in the neighbourhood, the first real incident between Tom Harte and his wife occurred. The woman was taking overly long at making herself up and Tom, being dressed and ready to go, was trying to chivvy her along. He had a pair of gloves in his hand and he came up behind her as she sat in front of the mirror.

'Hurry up now!' says he, striking her across the shoulders with the gloves, half in fun. 'Hurry along or we'll be late!'

The woman turned to him and in her green eyes was the same bitter coldness that he had seen on the day that he had first met her.

'That's once', she said with an edge to her voice. 'Twice more!'

And, suddenly, Tom remembered the agreement that they had made all that time before on the seashore. If he were to strike her three times, for any reason, then he would surely lose her. And he had struck her once already! Although he had only done it in jest, the woman had taken it very seriously indeed and for the rest of the night treated him with a lofty disdain. He went to the ball greatly chastened, but his wife never made reference to the incident again.

Time passed and the woman bore Tom Harte a child. And a grand and lovely child it was too, full of fun and laughter. It grew into a strapping toddler, filled with energy and vitality. Tom doted on it and took every opportunity that he could to play with it.

One afternoon they had all gone to the shore above Cushendun and were playing on the beach. Tom and the child were both in fine form, romping and squealing across the sand, but the woman kept her distance from them and remained seated on a nearby rock, preferring to work at her knitting. Tom was anxious that she should join in the fun and, with a wink to the child, he ran up to her with his hand raised.

'Join in our sport', he shouted, laughing, 'or I shall smack you.'

The child laughed with delight as Tom gave his wife a playful smack on the back of the hand. The woman, however, was not so amused. The deep coldness returned to her eyes as she stared up at her husband.

'That's twice!' she said evenly. 'Once more!'

Tom started to protest. After all, he had only smacked her to amuse the child. But she waved him away and refused to discuss the subject any further.

So it went on. As the child grew older, the woman became more and more difficult to live with and increasingly withdrew into herself. Late in the evening, Tom Harte would find her standing by the seashore looking out over the ocean in the last light of the day. When he came up to speak to her, she would turn away and go into the house, but he knew that she was pining for the world under the waves.

At last he couldn't stand her long silences any more. He walked down to the beach one evening, to where she was standing looking out across the incoming tide, and gripped her by her shoulders.

'What is the matter with you, woman?' he asked, almost at his wits end. 'You have ignored both me and our child and now you seem to spend all your time down by the ocean. You will not talk and you will not laugh with us. Your face is always gloomy and sour. What is it with you?'

The woman turned to him and her eyes were once more as cold as the depths.

'I promised, when we first met, that I would be a good wife to you', she said icily, 'and that I have been. I have cooked and sewed and looked after the house for you. I have raised your child. But I am a being of the ocean, not of the land, and I sometimes long to return there. I often think of the land far beneath the waves from where I came and of my own people who live there. When I think of it all I am very sad with my lot on the land. Is it not enough for you that I have married you and that I take care of you, mortal? Leave me to my own thoughts and trouble me no further.'

Her words stung Tom a little and, without thinking, he reached out and struck her in anger. He didn't strike her too hard and the anger was past in an instant, but it was enough.

'That's three times!' she cried with a sort of savage triumph. 'Now I can return to the sea! Farewell to the land!'

And, without turning to look at her husband, she went striding into the ocean and the water rose around her. Tom Harte made to run after her but she was walking too quickly and the sea was soon up to her shoulders. He had to draw back for fear of being drowned. The woman walked on and was soon lost to view. That was the last that he saw of her.

He lived for many years after that in the cottage by the sea. He never married again and the child which he raised became a great fisherman in his own right and his descendents still live in this area today. But there were moonlit nights when Tom Harte, even in his old age, would sit on the rocks above the village of Glenarm and look sadly out across the sea in the moonlight.''

The Dead

The dead have always played a central role in rural Irish folklore. Whether as insubstantial ghosts wandering through the countryside or walking corpses returning to torment the living, our former ancestors have always exercised an intense and continuing fascination for those who survive them and have formed the basis for many hair-raising tales. The dead, it appears, will not go away.

The belief in returning ghosts, spirits or corpses may have its origin in primitive ancestor worship. It was well known throughout the country that the dead had to be looked after at all times. Not to do so was to invite misfortune upon yourself, your family or your community. Nor has this belief wholly died out. In 1993, I spoke to an old man in north Cavan who claimed that, as a child, he remembered the corpse of his grandfather coming back from the grave on some nights during the winter months to sit at the fire and smoke a pipe of tobacco. He said that he also remembered actually touching the skin of the corpse and finding it very cold. His grandfather never spoke but sat warming himself by the fire. The rest of the family ignored this and went off to bed, leaving the corpse sitting in front of a good blaze. When they got up in the morning, I was told, the corpse was gone – presumably back to its grave. This story was borne out, without prompting, by one of the old gentleman's sisters.

A returning corpse also features in the following story, which comes from the Dublin mountains.

The Undead Priest

"There was a widow woman one time, lived away in a remote mountainous area outside Dublin. The place she lived in was very lonely and she had only one son who went into the priesthood. He was very intelligent and was away for years at the seminary in Maynooth. Never once did he come back to see his mother until he was quite old. They said that he had some sort of sickness about him and that he had come home to stay for a while with his old mother to recover his health.

She was very pleased to see him and made him very welcome. Her neighbours, too, called from time to time to welcome him home but he had been away for such a long time and was no longer a local man, nor did he make any attempt to become part of the community. He was sharp and aloof and, truth to tell, with all his book-learning he considered himself much better than those who lived in the district around. Local people consulted him on matters of faith but they did not socialise with him nor he with them. He simply shut himself away in his mother's cottage in the mountains with his books and his own thoughts. Then, just before his fiftieth birthday, he suddenly died. Whether it was because of what ailed him I don't know, but I believe that the death was very quick.

His body was laid out in his mother's house and everybody in the immediate locality called there to pay their respects and to help in the funeral. Indeed, it was a sad day when they waked him and a sadder day yet when they carried his coffin from the lonely mountain cottage to the rocky graveyard on the side of a hill a few miles away. All the people in the locality went to the funeral, but the mother was not feeling up to the long and difficult journey and so remained at home.

It took some time for the burial party to reach the graveyard, and the trip back over the uneven road was just as slow. Night was coming down and long shadows were beginning to fall before they came within sight of their own homes. As they came over the last hill, the mourners saw a man approaching them, walking very quickly. They looked at each other.

'Every man in the district has been at the funeral', said one. 'Who could that man be and why is he coming from that direction?'

The leaders signalled for the procession to stop and they stood by the roadside and waited as the walker drew level with them. As he neared, they all saw very clearly the face of the man that they had just buried!

He passed them on the other side of the road, still striding along swiftly at an almost inhuman speed, his head slightly turned away from them. Even so, they were able to make sure of his identity and they all saw the paleness of his skin, the hard and glittering wide-open eyes and the lips drawn back across his shrivelled gums as though caught in the rictus of death. And he was not wearing the winding sheet in which he had been buried but rather the decent, black frock-coat of a regular priest. He passed them by and disappeared around a bend in the road which led towards the graveyard.

When he had passed, the people in the procession began to talk fearfully among themselves, casting long glances along the road that he had taken. There was much discussion as to whether they should go to the mother's house, which lay about a mile distant, and tell her what they had seen. It was finally agreed that they should visit the grieving woman and check that she was well and settled for the night, but that nothing should be said about the apparition. So agreed, they went to the cottage, approaching the door and knocking loudly. There was no answer. Climbing up onto an upturned basin, one of the mourners peered through the kitchen window to see the old woman lying on the floor apparently in a dead faint. Using their shoulders, some of the neighbours broke down the door and gently lifted her, reviving her with a little whiskey which they had about them. Hesitantly, she told them what had happened.

About half-an-hour earlier there had been a knock on her door. She could not imagine who it might be since all her neighbours were at the funeral and she was rather afraid to answer it. The knock came again, this time more loudly and insistently. Getting up on a kitchen stool, the woman peered out of the small, high window. To her horror, she saw her dead son standing there in broad daylight, much as she had remembered him when he was alive.

Although he was not looking directly at her, she was still able to see the ghastly pallor of his skin and the awful wolfishness of his whole bearing. He seemed to be half-crouching as though preparing to spring upon her when she answered the door. Fear swept over her and she felt the stool give way beneath her feet as her legs buckled and she fainted. There she had lain until her neighbours had found her.

The undead priest was never seen in the neighbourhood again but people in that remote parish still pass his grave in the lonely mountain cemetery with a quick and fearful step."

Prominent amongst those who returned from the dead were debtors or mothers who had died in childbirth. There was a widespread country saying that "a man who dies owing money or a woman who leaves a newly-born child will never rest quiet

in the grave", and there are many traditional stories of walking
corpses who have returned to place their finances in order or to
see the children whom they left behind them in the world.
Sometimes, too, a dead mother might come back to view her
offspring with a more sinister purpose in mind, as is this old tale
from County Sligo.

The Woman without her Boots

"This story is true for the man that it happened to was a full
cousin of the person who told it to me, and he swore to it on his
mother's own soul, God rest her.

There was a man named Hennessy that lived in the townland
of Ballybron. He was a quiet, decent sort of fellow but he was
married to a sly, awkward woman. Ellen Lydon her name was
and she was a thin, red-headed woman with a very bad tongue in
her head.

Anyway, after they had been married for two or three years,
the wife died suddenly, giving birth to a wee boy. She was buried
in the old churchyard at Drumcoolin. Now, you might know
that this old graveyard is a very dark and evil-looking place.
There is a ruined church there and the cemetery is overgrown
and badly kept. Local people say that it is haunted both by
ghosts and by the fairies, for there is a fairy bush on its very edge.
They have now stopped using it as a resting place, I think, and
Hennessy's wife was one of the last to be buried there.

After her passing, Hennessy kept the child at home close by
him and brought another woman to his house to help bring him
up. But the other woman couldn't look after the child all that
well. She couldn't take him on the breast for she had no milk of
her own to give him. The wee boy became thin and sickly-

looking and was not doing well at all.

A few weeks went by. Then, one night, the husband was wakened by a sudden noise in the scullery of his cottage. He got up in the dark and went to look, imagining it to be a cat or some animal that had got in. But there at the back of the scullery was his former wife going through the drawers of an old cupboard looking for a crust of bread. It was quite dark but he could see the redness of her hair in the moonlight which streamed in through the kitchen window. As his eyes became more accustomed to the gloom he was able to make her out more distinctly. He saw that she was just as he had remembered her, only she was dressed in a winding sheet and was barefoot.

She paid him no heed but went on looking through the drawer until at last she found a bit of crust and snatched it up and ate it like a wild thing. Even then, she did not appear to see him but walked over to where her child lay in the cradle. Lifting the wee one she took it on the breast and fed it. The child sucked contentedly without waking and, when it was finished, the dead mother laid it in the cradle again. Then she gave a loud sigh and turned towards the door.

Hennessy, who had been watching all the time, was terrified. He tried to speak but the words seemed to stick in his throat and he couldn't utter a sound. The dead woman let herself out into the night and went off across the fields towards the ruined church at Drumcoolin. Standing at the door, Hennessy watched her go until she was lost to his sight. Then he went back in to look at the child who was sleeping peacefully. You can bet with certainty that he didn't get another wink of sleep that night!

And the next night, the dead woman came again. She lifted the latch and let herself in and, after hunting through the kitchen once more, ate a piece of cheese that Hennessy had left out on a plate. Then she went back to the cradle and lifted the child once again and fed it. Hennessy had got up by this time and stood watching her as she went through all this and, though he was fairly shaking with fear, he found his voice at last.

'What are you doing here, Ellen?' he asked, terrified, but the woman never answered him and went on feeding the child. As on the previous night, he was not sure that she saw him at all with those strange, dead eyes. Then, laying the wee boy back in the cradle, she turned upon her heel and went out again into the dark.

This happened for a good few nights. All the while, the child prospered and throve the very best. It put on weight and was happy and healthy because it was getting milk from the breast. Hennessy, however, was frightened and although he asked his dead wife a number of times what she was doing, she never answered him. And each night she was dressed just the same, in her winding-sheet and completely barefoot.

She had been coming each night for well over a week when her manner seemed to change. One night Hennessy saw that she hadn't lifted the child, which was now plump and healthy-looking, but was just standing looking down at it. Without touching it, she turned again and went out into the dark, back to Drumcoolin. This time, Hennessy was really frightened for he thought that he now knew what the corpse's purpose might be. It had been fattening the child up to take him back to the cold grave at Drumcoolin! He shuddered at the very thought.

There was a woman living over near Castle Taylor, an aunt of Murty Devlin's, and she was very knowledgeable about ghosts and fairies and Hennessy went to her to ask her advice. She listened gravely to what he told her.

'Tell me how she was dressed', she said at last, drawing on her pipe. Hennesy told her. The old woman nodded.

'And she had no boots upon her feet?' she enquired. Hennessy confirmed that she hadn't. Murty Devlin's aunt thought for a long while.

'The next time she comes', she answered, 'ask her in the name of God why she has no boots on her feet. Because you have used the holy name, she must answer you and must answer truthfully. Then we'll have the measure of her and I'll instruct you further. Only ask her quickly for if you don't she will take the child with her, back to Drumcoolin, and you'll never see him again. That was surely her purpose in fattening him up from her breast.'

Although greatly frightened, Hennessy got up the following night, just as the corpse came in. The dead woman made no attempt to search for food as she had done on previous nights but simply went and stood above the cradle, looking down at the sleeping child.

'In the name of God, Ellen', choked out Hennessy, naming her, 'why are you without your boots?'

Now, because he had asked the question in the name of God, she could answer him and she had to answer truthfully, just as Murty Devlin's aunt had said.

'I am without my boots because there are nails in them', says she, in a hollow voice. Then, before he could ask her anything else, she turned and was gone. With this answer Hennessy went back to Murty Devlin's aunt and told her what the corpse had said.

'It's as I thought', she nodded. 'Now we know how to keep her from the cradle until the boy is grown.'

She went over to a blacksmith's shop which stood near her home and brought back an iron nail which had never shod a horse.

'Put this around the neck of the child', said Murty Devlin's aunt, 'and you'll be plagued no more by the walking dead.'

And that was the way of it. The man tied the nail on a piece of string and put it round the wee boy's neck and he never saw the corpse of his former wife again. She feared the iron in the nail, do you see? It was the iron nails around the sole of her boot that made her leave them off and go barefoot. Neither corpses nor fairies can have anything to do with the blacksmith's iron.

The boy grew up well and good and was a farmer in the area and his sons are still living there. Now, I know that the story is true for it was Niall Finnegan who told it to me himself and the man that it happened to was a full cousin of his own."

Irish tradition has it that the fairies were charged by God to make sure that deserving souls reached the gates of heaven which they (the fairies) were not allowed to enter themselves. The roads in some country areas were therefore thronged, usually around November, with the souls of those who had died in the district within the last year, all making their way to their reward in the hereafter.

This gave rise to the notion of the "fairy funeral", a procession of wailing souls along the darkened roads which the fairies both guided and guarded. The Good People conducted this task reluctantly and in bad humour, for they were being denied entrance to heaven whilst mortal souls were being admitted. Consequently to meet one of these processions on the road was to court disaster. The fairies had the power to take the unwary along with them into the after-life, in which case the individual would be found dead by the roadside the following morning, or to inflict some ghastly task upon those whom they encountered, such as carrying a shrouded corpse or a coffin on their backs.

There were certain charms which could be employed to avoid this. Margaret Gallagher from south Fermanagh told me that her grandfather, Pat Gallagher, had met a fairy funeral on the road one night near the village of Belcoo and had known what to say – "My face to you, my back from you" – and they passed him by without seeing him. However, he kept his face turned away and didn't see any of the souls of his neighbours who walked the road with the fairies that night. He was lucky for, as the following story from the border country of Cavan shows, not all travellers were so fortunate.

The Fairy Funeral at Killycreen

"In the townland of Killycreen, just on the border between Fermanagh and Cavan, there used to be a field that was given over to the burying of suicides and unbaptised infants. It lay directly on the border and there was a stile there set into a stone wall that marked the crossing from Fermanagh into Cavan. A man called Hugh Maguire owned this field and it was an extremely dangerous place to cross at night for the souls of those who take their own lives or who die without baptism are denied entrance to heaven and they sometimes wait in lonely places close to their graves, seeking a way back into the world. So it was at Killycreen.

It was a great place for the fairy funerals too. Woe betide the man who met the fairy funeral upon the road after the sun had gone down for he might be taken along with it and made to carry a corpse or a coffin upon his back.

There was a cousin of my own, one of the Maguires that lived over in Cavan, was crossing the fields there. It was late one night near Halloweve and he came up to the stile and made to jump over it. And, as he did so, didn't he find himself right back on the road again. There were two other men with him, neither of whom he knew, and each of them was carrying a dark wooden coffin on his back. My cousin had a coffin on his own back as well, and he was walking along the road carrying it. No matter how he tried, he couldn't put it down, nor whatever way he turned, he couldn't leave the road but just kept on walking straight ahead.

Looking around him, he saw that he was walking along the road towards the field where they buried the unbaptised infants and, the more he thought about it, the coffin on his back indeed felt as if it might contain the body of a child. Such children often become the property of the fairies who are charged with their burial around the dark time of the year. He knew then that this was a fairy funeral, and that he was in the middle of it and there wasn't a thing that he could do about it. He just kept walking onwards as if in some sort of trance. In fact, the whole situation seemed very much like a dream to him. He couldn't help himself at all for his body wouldn't obey him.

Along the road, he passed by a house belonging to a neighbour, a Mrs Nixon. As he went by her door, he shouted out to her to come down and save him. But she was in her bed, her house was in darkness and her door was barred and bolted for the night and she couldn't have heard him anyway, for people who have had a scare with the fairies can never be heard. The house remained shuttered and closed against his cries. There was no help to be had there and he passed by her door and on into the dark.

Just before the turn of the road he met two other neighbours that he knew coming walking up towards Wheathill, but neither of them saw him for the fairy glamour was on him and he was invisible to their eyes. They passed him by and went on their way down the road.

The funeral took him to the gate of the field where the children were buried and turned into it. With slow steps, he himself turned from the road in through the gateway. The weight of the coffin on his back appeared to lighten slightly as he walked across the grass. Then he came to a stop, close to a large and shadowy tree in the far corner of the field.

The minute he did so, he found himself back over the fields again where he had been before. Indeed, he was standing on the other side of the stile that he'd been trying to cross, and was now in County Cavan. It was early morning with the sun touching the hills and the first dew of the morning was on his coat. But he knew for a certainty that he'd been away with the fairies all night and that he'd been made to carry a child's coffin. Crossing himself at the very thought of it, he hurried home and went straightaway to morning Mass in case he was still touched by the fairy magic.

Later on, however, he went back to Killycreen and looked around the field. Away in a corner, under a large tree, he thought that he saw a small, strangely-shaped depression on the ground. It looked indeed as if a tiny coffin might have been buried there.

There was great talk in the countryside after that about a baby that had been stillborn to a woman over by Derrygonnelly and it might have been its coffin that my cousin had been made to carry that night for it would have died without the benefit of priest or clergy. He thought that was the way of it but he could never be sure."

Away with the Fairies

Who are the fairies? The Book of Armagh *claims that they are the old gods of the earth. Other sources say that they are the remnants of an old race, the Tuatha de Danaan, which came to Ireland in the mists of pre-history. Other ancient texts claim that they are fallen angels, not good enough to remain with God, nor evil enough to be consigned to hell with Lucifer and his demons, so they inhabit the dark places of the mortal world.*

Relationships between the Good People (fairies) and mortals have never been easy. Fairies disliked humans for two reasons. Firstly, mortals enjoyed a relationship with God which they did not. Second, the fairies had once made an agreement with the wily St Patrick that the earth should be divided between the human and fairy races. The humans should inhabit all the places which sunlight touched and the fairies would have the rest. The Good People were therefore consigned to the lands under the earth and the remote and lightless glens and valleys amongst the mountains. Too late, they realised what they had agreed to and this unfair division has since remained a source of animosity between them and the sons of Adam.

It was the fervent hope of the fairies that they would one day re-enter heaven but because they did not have any human blood in their veins, God had turned His back on them. They believed that if they had but one drop, they would be as assured of salvation as any mortal. Consequently, fairies tried to lure mortals into their own realm, perhaps to mate with them and so produce offspring with human blood. Instances of humans being carried away by the fairy host, of being "away with the fairies", therefore form the basis of many folktales. Sometimes these people returned home after a period of time (seven years is common) when the fairies had grown tired of them; sometimes they never returned at all.

In many tales, it was through the acceptance of fairy hospitality that the mortal became trapped within their world. If carried away by the fairy host, it was therefore imperative not to eat or drink anything whilst in their company, otherwise they would have unlimited power over you. This prohibition forms the basis of this folktale from County Roscommon.

Jemmy Doyle in the Fairy House

"You will no doubt have heard of my grandfather, Jemmy Doyle. He was always travelling between the ceili houses, reciting stories and singing songs, for he was a great entertainer. And there was no man who could down a tumbler of poteen like him. Ah, he was a well-known man indeed.

One evening, he was coming home from a fair near Castlereagh. It was a night at the end of summer, about ten o'clock, when it was just starting to get dark. He was travelling along a long and lonely road between the hills but he had walked it many times before and he wasn't afraid of it, even in the half-light. Truth to tell, he had probably been in a pub at the fair or at a shebeen along the way and had a sup or two of drink upon him. And yet, my grandfather insists that he was perfectly sober that night.

However, as he came to a turn in the road, he suddenly came upon a large house standing in a clump of trees a little way back from the road where no house should be. My grandfather wracked his brains but he couldn't think of a house having been built there – and such a grand house as well. Surely he would have heard about it! Still, it had been a little while since he had been on this stretch of road and it was always possible that somebody *had* built a dwelling there. All the same, he was fairly taken by the size and splendour of it.

Indeed, the house was as splendid as if it belonged to a country gentleman, and every window in it was lit up with lights of varying colours. Its doors lay open and the light from inside streamed out onto the roadway and, as my grandfather stopped to look, he heard music coming from a ceili that was going on there. The tunes were so lively that he couldn't help but tap his feet on the roadway, and the laughter that flooded out was so jolly that he couldn't help but join in.

Never one to miss a ceili or a gathering of any description, he went up and peered in round the doorpost. He found himself looking into a large, grand hall which was filled with richly-dressed gentlemen and ladies, all eating and drinking. They were dressed in a very old style and moved stiffly and with courtly bows to each other. The hall was lined with tables filled with meat and drink of the very best, so full of food, in fact, that they almost groaned under the very weight of it. And away at the far end of the hall sat a number of pipers, fiddlers, harpers and bodhran players, all playing away at wild, old tunes that my grandfather remembered as a boy. Everywhere, silks and tapestries were hanging and lamps were blazing, giving the hall a very cheery air. Indeed, so merry did the company seem that my grandfather took several steps into the hall, as if to join in the revelry.

Just then, one of the grandly-dressed men, seated at the head of one of the tables, looked up and saw him.

'Come in, come in, Mr Doyle', he cried. 'You are most welcome here for our ceili is open to all.'

My grandfather very hesitantly took another couple of steps into the hall but the man beckoned him further with a great gusto and the ladies in their silk dresses rustled their fans and made cow's eyes at him, smiling shyly to themselves. Now, Jemmy Doyle, never one to neglect the eye of a pretty girl or a glass of poteen, came forward to the table.

'Sit down, Mr Doyle, sit down', the grandly-dressed man encouraged him. 'Sit down and have a sup with us for this is a grand gathering, is it not?'

'Indeed it is', replied my grandfather and he took his seat at the table.

This, of course, was a fairy house and if my grandfather truly had had his wits about him he would have continued on his way home and would have had nothing to do with the Gentry (fairies) that were gathered there. But, as I said earlier, he might have had a drop of drink on him and this made him bold. Nevertheless, he had the wit not to take any of the meat or poteen that was offered to him right away but was content to sit and listen to the music, for he had an ear for a fine tune.

'Will you not take a glass of spirits with us?' the man asked him, holding out a bottle invitingly, but my grandfather waved it away with an excuse.

'Ah no indeed, your honour', he said civilly. 'If you let me listen to these grand tunes, I'll have a sup with you by and by.'

The man offered him some meat from a plate but my grandfather, who in all truth wasn't very hungry, declined that just as politely. He listened for a while, tapping his foot to old and merry melodies and he was having a grand time altogether.

But occasionally the fairy man would offer him meat and drink in so friendly a manner that at last my grandfather couldn't refuse any longer. He held out a glass and had it filled with poteen.

He was just about to raise it to his lips when, looking along the table, he saw a man sitting next to him. Lord preserve us, wasn't it his neighbour who'd been dead for twenty years! The sight of the dead man startled my grandfather so much that he froze where he was, with the drink half-way to his lips. The corpse, however, raised a warning finger.

'Eat or drink nothing that they offer you', it said in a voice that was so low that my grandfather could barely hear it. 'Or else you will never be able to leave this house and they will have you in their power forever. That is the way with the Good People.'

Then it turned back to its own plate.

With this warning, my grandfather set down the poteen tumbler again, watching it fixedly as if it were the deadliest poison. The grand gentleman leaned forward a little in his seat.

'Are you not drinking with us, Mr Doyle?' said he, a trifle anxiously. 'I guarantee that you will not get finer meat or drink anywhere in Ireland.'

He said this, you see, so that my grandfather would drink and fall into the fairy power. But Jemmy Doyle shook his head, although the sweat was fairly breaking upon his brow.

'Ah, indeed, your honour speaks truly', he answered with a slight shake in his voice. 'I am neither hungry nor thirsty at this moment, but I shall sup a bit presently.' And he sat back once more to listen to the music.

The fairy man was not to be turned, however, and suddenly stood up before the assembled company, raising his own tumbler in a toast.

'Here's health, long life and good fortune to our honoured guest, Mr Jemmy Doyle', he cried, taking a swallow of the poteen. The others raised their glasses in response and looked towards my grandfather for his reply to such a grand toast. He rose, with the poteen glass in his hand, and raised it slowly. The eyes of all the Good People around him watched hungrily.

'Your honour', Jemmy began, 'I am a humble man with few possessions ...' The grandly-dressed man smiled and nodded, waiting for my grandfather to take a swallow from the glass. Jemmy, however, raised the tumbler and dashed it against the flags of the floor, '... but, in God's holy name, I'll not let you take what I hold most dear – my own soul!'

The poteen glass exploded in a plume of smoke and the Good People all around fairly screamed with rage. A great wind swept through the house and seemed to gather my grandfather up in it. It threw him against a table and he remembered no more.

He opened his eyes to find himself lying by the side of the road, a little way back and just below a thick clump of trees. It was early morning, just after cock-crow, and there was not a sign of the grand house in which he had spent the night anywhere nearby. He was stiff and aching and there was a faint taste of poteen in the back of his mouth. Getting to his feet, he looked around him and saw that he was actually lying close to the foot of a whitethorn bush, which is well known throughout the countryside as a sacred fairy bush. A great fear and trembling came on him and he hurried home and went straight away to the priest to make confession for fear he was still tainted by fairy magic.

For a while afterwards my grandfather became very sober and temperate in his behaviour, though after a year or so had passed and the fear of the experience had diminished, he went back to his old habits of drinking, singing and story-telling. But he never encountered the Good People again. That's the truth of it for it was himself that told the story often."

Fairies and the dead were closely linked in Irish folktales. Departed friends frequently warn the living against accepting fairy hospitality and so save them from being "taken away". However, mortals sometimes blunder into the fairy world with disastrous consequences: witless humans attach themselves to fairy processions or cavalcades; others take up with individual fairies. Such an instance forms the basis for the next tale from County Down. First of all, however, I must say a word about the pooka.

The pooka was a particularly mischievous fairy sprite and almost every misfortune that befell an individual during the hours of darkness could be laid at its door. It took a variety of shapes. Sometimes it went about as an evil, dark and misshapen goblin, sometimes as a huge eagle with hooked and rending claws and sometimes as a giant goat with long, curling horns. Most often, though, it appeared as a terrifying black horse with flaming eyes and a long, flowing mane, snorting its sulphurous breath into the night air. It galloped past houses, roaring fiercely and belching stinking smoke as it did so, terrifying the good Christian people who were, no doubt, in thier beds. It also leapt upon the backs of unwary travellers and, only by blessing themselves three times in succession, could they free themselves from its evil influence.

The Irish king, Brian Boru, was the first man to bring it under control and he did this by putting a bridle on it, made from three hairs from the pooka's tail. He then climbed upon its back and rode it until it was exhausted. But the Irish ruler was not the only human to sit on the pooka's back. Some other mortals have also done so with much more terrible results, as any storyteller in the Mournes will relate.

Robbie the Rake and the Pooka

"There was a pooka, one time, that made its home under the Pooka's Bridge and the bridge is still there, up by Aughnahoorey. Well, you could see him on any night of the week, grazing away down in the glen under the span of the bridge in the moonlight. But, although it was a very fine animal, nobody would go near it for they were all frightened of the fairy magic that might be about it. The pooka was left very much in peace to get on with its grazing. It never bothered a soul in the district and they never bothered it.

Now there was a man in that locality by the name of Robbie the Rake that lived over in Ballykeel, and he was a wild and drunken sort of boy altogether. There was no house where there was drinking or ceili-ing or card-playing going on that this Robbie didn't visit on his travels. This night, he was coming back from his ceili across the Pooka's Bridge and was a bit the worse for the drink. When he reached the middle of the bridge itself, didn't the drink trip him up and he fell over the side and right onto the pooka's back. Well, it took both of them by surprise and the fairy animal gave a wild neighing and took off helter-skelter with Robbie holding onto its mane for grim death.

Up hill and down brae they went, through briars and bushes, lintholes and loanings. They landed, pell-mell, on the top of Slieve Binian and then onto Knockree above Mourne Park. The people looked from their windows to see Robbie flying past at a terrible speed, for the pooka can travel much faster than any normal horse. The poor fellow shouted out to them in his distress but before they had time to do anything, the pooka was gone again and Robbie with it. All they saw was the white blur of Robbie's face as he whistled by them, quick as the wind, in a mad dash.

From Mourne Park, the pooka raced on to Mill Bay, trailing poor Robbie through mud and slime, over whins and rocks, until all his clothes were torn and his hands and face were badly scratched. The branches of trees tore at his coat and pulled the shirt from his back, and whatever money he had in his pockets was scattered cross the fields behind them. On and on they went, as far as the old castle at Greencastle and, by that time, all the drink had left Robbie and the cold sweat was fairly dripping off him. But he couldn't let go of the pooka's mane, so he stayed where he was and took all the bumps and scratches that the fairy creature gave him.

Well, at long and at last, they reached Dunavel Fort and here the pooka threw Robbie off and landed him right in the middle of the fort itself. He lay on the ground there, quite sure that the fairy beast was going to trample and kill him after all. It rose up above him and its hooves passed across him like a shadow. Just at this moment, the big clock away down in Kilkeel struck twelve o'clock and when it heard that, the pooka gave another loud nikker and raised its hooves even higher to paw at the air.

Although he was battered, bruised and exhausted from his wild travels, Robbie threw up his hands to save himself for he was sure that he was going to be trampled to death. The pooka, however, took off back to Aughnahoorey in a puff of smoke and left Robbie lying where he was. He had to make his own way home and a long way it was. And, furthermore, his clothes were so ripped and torn that he had barely the shred of a shirt to cover his decency. He made his way along the sheughs and hedges, ducking down behind walls and bushes in case his neighbours would see the state of him. Indeed, it took long weeks and months for all the scrapes and bruises to heal and, for years after, he was still a bit stiff when he walked any distance. It was some years too before the pooka was seen again, grazing in the moonlight under the bridge.

Well, from that night until the day he died, Robbie never left his own house after nightfall. He became very sober and straight in his ways and he stayed well away from the ceili-ing in the country houses. He had learned his lesson all right. But, as he said himself afterwards, it was all bad enough but not nearly as bad as a bad marriage. So a bad marriage must be a shocking thing indeed!"

Many stories concerning encounters with fairies involved card-playing. Country morality was often outraged at the drinking and gambling that went on in some ceili-houses and built prohibitions against these vices into its folklore. This tale, from north Antrim, comprises many of these warnings. It comes from around the Dervock-Bushmills area where it is still well known.

The Fairy Gamblers

"There was a young man named Dan MacKillop who lived near Bushmills in my grandmother's time and he was said to have been a very wild buck indeed. He was a great man for the wagers and they say that he would have a bet on two flies climbing on a wall, just for the sport of it. He was also very fond of the drink. Now, this was at a time when people gathered in one house or another for a drink and a smoke and a bit of crack and there wasn't a house in the whole countryside that young MacKillop wasn't in. Every night he would be running from one house to another.

This Halloweve night he had been in a house over in Dervock and was walking back along the road home to Bushmills. It was a great, moonlit night and there was a bit of frost in the air, but young MacKillop was well fortified from the chill for he had the poteen in him. Well, with that in him he was afraid of nothing that he might meet.

Near Bushmills didn't he fall in with these other two boys who were running between the houses in search of amusement. He didn't know either of them but they had a bottle of the mountain spirit with them and one of them offered him a drink. He fell into step with them and soon they were laughing and yarning as though they'd known each other for years.

'I know a house that we can have a game of cards in', says one.

Now this was like music to young MacKillop's ears and he asked if he could come along.

'Have ye money?' asks the other and when Dan MacKillop said that he had, they linked arms with him and took him along with them.

They walked and walked, well away from the Dervock road and away into the mountains. They walked along roads that were no more than stone tracks across the hills and Dan MacKillop slipped and fell a couple of times, for the stones were wet with the frost and if it hadn't been for the other two, he'd have done himself an injury. At last they came to a small whitewashed cottage standing in a hollow in the hills. The only light that came from the windows was that of candles and, through the open door, young MacKillop could see a great fire of peat sods roaring in the hearth. The young men ducked under the doorway and went in, with Dan MacKillop following.

The inside of the cottage was quite bare. It had a dirt floor and in the middle of the room stood a rough wood table with four chairs around it. There was an old mountainy man sitting on the other side of it, eating something from a tin plate with a long horn spoon. He looked ancient, long and whiskery, dressed in a blouse of bleached linen and a shabby pair of white freize trousers. He wore a soft dark hat on his head which put his face almost completely into darkness in the pale candlelight.

'Save you kindly, Lannihan of the Mountain', said one of the young men as they came in. The old man scraped his plate and looked up at them with a long, lonely stare.

'Save you all!' said he in a strange, hollow voice that seemed to come from the roots of the earth itself. 'Come in and sit in the heat for it's a cold night surely.'

Now, young MacKillop should have been afraid of this isolated place and of the strange old man but the drink that he had in him had made him bold. He came in and sat down at the rough table. The old man got up and went to a dresser in the corner, from which he produced four glasses. Opening another bottle of mountain spirits, he poured them each a glass.

For a while the talk was general. The old man spoke of failed crops and lost sheep and the mists which drifted continually across the mountains, talking in his deep, booming voice, which sounded like the wind in the tall trees. Then the talk turned to gambling, and Lannihan of the Mountain went back to the dresser and brought out a pack of greasy, pasteboard cards and put them on the table.

'If you have a mind for playin' the cards', he said in his

timeless, far-away voice, 'we can have a game now.'

At first, young MacKillop protested, for the drink and the heat from the fire were making him sleepy, but the others produced their money and he couldn't resist. Lannihan of the Mountain lit a tall candle in a great, carved holder and placed it on the edge of the table.

'We'll play for as long as it takes the candle to burn down', he said. 'After that it'll be morning.'

He shuffled the cards with such speed that Dan MacKillop, his eyes heavy with drink, could not follow him. Then the old man dealt.

'All the riches of the world have been played for and lost over these cards', said Lannihan of the Mountain with a great sadness in his voice. 'I ask you again, do you want a game?'

MacKillop looked at his hand and it was a good one. He nodded eagerly.

So they began to play. At first the game went Dan MacKillop's way, although the pot was small. But the crack around the table was good and each of his wins was taken with good humour by the others. MacKillop raked in more money and won a few more hands. His glass was filled more times than he counted and it was the smoothest and sweetest poteen that he had ever tasted. He wanted to ask the old man where he had got it but, amongst the mountain people, nobody ever asks the source of poteen. So he played on. The candle on the edge of the table flickered but never seemed to burn down very far.

The game then went to one of the other young men for a while but then it came back to Dan MacKillop. He scraped his money to him and called for another game. Lannihan of the Mountain dealt another hand.

As the money in the pot increased, the old mountainy man dug in the pocket of his trousers and pulled out an ancient silver coin, worn smooth through years of use. This he threw into the centre of the table as a stake. The old coin winked and twinkled in the candlelight.

Now the game turned to Lannihan of the Mountain and the old man won the next half-dozen hands. Dan MacKillop began to lose patience with the way that the play was going. It had been all right so long as he was winning but now he was losing, and losing heavily. With each hand, Lannihan of the Mountain tossed the old silver coin into the pot where it lay winking and twinkling, tempting the young man.

'Sure that may be his luck and all!' thought young MacKillop and he resolved to win the coin from the old man, no matter what it took.

His bets grew wilder and wilder and every time he lost. Lannihan of the Mountain scooped up the pot in his horny hands and each time he took the old coin with it. The other two players had by this time dropped out of the game, becoming little more than shadows beside the fire. The wager was now between Dan MacKillop and the old mountain man.

MacKillop would not give up for the old coin fascinated him, like an evil eye, and he was determined to win it. And still it eluded him. No matter how good a hand he thought he had, the old man was always able to beat it, but the young fellow wagered away, still trying to get his hands on it. One of the others filled his glass again and the heat from the fire made him very drowsy.

At last he had gambled away all his money and had nothing left to wager with. He took off his ring and threw it into the centre of the table. Now this was a wedding ring which his grandmother, a very saintly woman, had left to him in her will and it had been blessed by a minister at the time of the wedding.

However, so anxious was he to win the coin that he put it up against the old man's money.

Lannihan of the Mountain looked at it with a long, long stare.

'It is too good a thing to lose in a game of cards', says he. 'Are you sure that you want to wager it?'

'In the name of God', replied MacKillop, 'though it was my grandmother's own ring, I'll put it against your money!' And he banged his fist on the table.

That was the last thing that he remembered doing, for the drink overtook him and he fell forward in a stupor.

He woke to find himself lying on the side of a mountain path in a part of the country that he didn't know. It was morning and there was a frost on his coat. Putting his hand in his pocket, he found that all his money had gone but that his grandmother's ring was still there. Getting up, he looked all around him and saw that he had been lying on the very edge of a fairy rath and that there was no sign of the building in which he had gambled the previous night. There were the walls of some old famine cottages away across the glen, to be sure, but he saw nothing of the whitewashed cottage anywhere nearby.

He had a fierce drouth on him and he drunk from a stream which gushed from among some stones. Then he set out to find out where he was.

He was on the other side of Carnkirk Mountain and it wasn't too hard to find his way back to the Dervock Road. He walked on and soon came to the borders of his own townland. There he met some people who were going to church for it was a Sunday morning. He didn't know one of them and they looked at him very strangely.

As he approached his own home he found that everything had changed. Ten years had passed since he had last left his own door and they had passed in a single night with the fairies. His father and mother had died in the meantime and, as he was an only child, the farm had been sold to an uncle who didn't want him about. I heard that he became a bit of a travelling man, tramping the roads all over the North of Ireland, making his living at bits and pieces of jobs here and there. His hair had turned very white and stayed that way until the day he died. He was never very well after that and he never gambled again, nor would he touch a drop of drink.

Ah, there's a lesson in that for us all. Never drink nor play cards at a ceili for you never know who you might be wagering with. That was the story that my grandmother told me anyway. There are still MacKillops living about the area near Bushmills, though I don't know if they are the same ones."

The Cry of the Banshee

No supernatural creature is better known in Irish folklore than the banshee. The name derives from the Irish bean sidhe *(woman of the fairy) but, although the banshee is invariably female, there is much argument as to whether or not she is strictly a fairy. Although generally regarded as one of the* sidhe *(fairy beings), she may also be a vengeful ghost or a warning ancestral spirit or, indeed, she may be human. The stories and legends told about the banshee often reflect this confusion.*

Whether she be human, fairy or ghost, there is no doubt that the banshee wails at an Irish death. Her cry was usually said to be that of the Irish keen – a low, wailing shout, full of melancholy, somewhere between the shriek of a she-fox and the moan of an owl. Sometimes it was said to be a sweet resonance, sometimes a hideous scream. Those who heard it were often filled with an inexplicable dread.

There appears to have been chiefly two types of banshee: a beautiful young woman who sang sweetly, and a hideous old hag who screeched out her warning. The former was popularly thought to be good and kind, her call welcoming the deceased into the land of the spirits, whilst the other was believed to be a malignant being, rejoicing in the passing of a human being.

Two tales, one from the Glens of Antrim, the other from Rathlin Island, tell of the banshee. In one story she is seen while in the other she is merely heard, but in both her call provokes an undoubted sense of dread.

Johnny Hegarty's

"We were all down at Johnny Hegarty's for a night's crack. That's Johnny's over by Glenshesk, you understand. There was always a drop of strong drink to be had at his house and there was always good crack too. It was a great gathering house for people from miles about through the Glens and from the island.

We were all sitting around. Johnny had a great fire of peats on and there was a good drop of the poteen on the go. There was a young fellow, one of the Craigs, with us from over on Rathlin. He had come over with a boat crew and had stayed behind for the night's jollification. Although Johnny had a grand fire on and the turf was burning well, young Craig complained of being cold but once he had a drop of the poteen in him, he seemed to come to himself again and join in the joviality. We were all in good form and telling old stories and there was a man, Neil McAuley, who was playing on the tin whistle. All was going well.

Then, just above the sound of the whistle, we all heard this long, thin, discordant and drawn-out cry, and there was a loud rap on the window of the cottage. The cry was repeated and we stopped our music and chat. The sound seemed to come from somewhere close by, so Johnny Hegarty himself got up and went over to the window to see what it was.

Now, you know Johnny, he was a big, tall man and if anybody was carrying on outside he would have fairly put the fear into them. When he looked through the glass, however, he jumped back with a shout for there was a face looking directly in at him. It was the face of an old, old woman, with big, wide staring eyes, like those of a fish, and a look that was strange and twisted. The skin was as pale as that of a corpse and the whole head was covered by some sort of green caul. Even as we looked at her, she opened her mouth and let a screech out of her. Her teeth were long and pointed, like those of a wild animal, that's the truth of it for I saw it myself. When Johnny looked again, there was nothing there, only the dark of the night and his own reflection in the glass. We all got to our feet and young Craig said that he felt a cold wind all through the place, even though there was a good peat fire roaring in the hearth.

Johnny thought that it might have been some tinker-woman that had been passing, peering in at the window to see what she could see, and that she had been surprised by us all sitting about the fire. He thought that she had ducked down by the outside wall and that she might still be there. We all went out to have a look and see if we could catch her but, even though we searched way beyond the turf-stack, there was nobody there at all. We went back in again and found that young Craig had not come with us but that he was still by the fire, still shivering from the unexplained chill. We knew then that it was the banshee that we had seen and heard and that Craig was 'marked' for death by her cry. We were all terribly afraid.

It turned out to be true enough, for a couple of days later the young man went out fishing on the rocks off Raughery and was swept away by the sea. They never found his body. That's a true story for I was there when it all happened and I seen and heard the banshee myself. But it was a good while ago."

The second story concerns someone who only heard the banshee, on Rathlin, but the effect was just as frightening. This story is told by the late Frank Craig, a Rathlin man himself:

The Banshee in the Bog

"I have never heard or seen the banshee myself but I know plenty that have. My uncle, Neil Craig, heard her cry on the island one time.

It appears that a man called Christie, that lived on the upper end of the island, took very ill late one night and was likely to die, and my uncle had to go for the priest. Now, the priest on Rathlin at that time was a man from the mainland. He was a youngish man, not used to the island ways, and he was lodging over by Tony McCauig's place. Well, my uncle went and got the clergyman all right and they set out for the upper end as quickly as they could.

It was a sharp, moonlit night and the land round about was as clear as if it had been daylight. On the way up to Christie's house they passed through a low, boggy place where the mist was rising off the mosses. From somewhere out across the bog, my uncle heard a strange, keening sound, starting off like a moan but becoming more shrill and then rising almost to a shriek, like a woman in great sorrow or torment. He looked all around him but he couldn't tell where it came from, for it seemed to come from everywhere and nowhere at once. Then he knew that it was the call of the banshee and that she was crying for Christie. He looked at the priest but the other gave no signal that he had heard it.

'What was that, Father?' my uncle asked. 'I thought that I heard something out in the mosses yonder!'

'Walk on', said the priest stiffly, 'for I hear nothing!' He couldn't let on that he had heard it on account of his holy office.

They walked on a piece further and the cry came again, thin and moaning, from somewhere out in the misty boglands. My uncle looked hard but, although the countryside was well lit by a huge and yellow moon, he still saw nothing.

'Do you hear it, Father?' he asked the priest.

'I heard nothing!' answered the other but there was a shake in his voice that let my uncle know that he *had* heard it. And the cry came again, rolling and swelling over the tufts of rushes and the watery sinkholes that marked the bog all around them.

'Don't you hear it?' asked my uncle, who was by now badly afraid. But the priest shook his head.

'It is the cry of a bird or a vixen out in the bog', said he. 'Pay it no heed!'

They went on and the sound died away behind them. When they got to Christie's place, the man was already dead.

So, after everything was done, my uncle had to leave the priest back again to Tony McCauig's. A bit of a mist had come up for it was near morning, but they went back the way that they had come and crossed the bog road again with my uncle's heart fairly stopping as they went, but they never heard another sound, only the stirring of the nightwind among the rushes.

When they got back to Tony's, the priest brought my uncle inside the house and said to the housekeeper, 'Give this man a glass of whiskey.'

A glass of whiskey was brought and my uncle drunk it down with the one swallow. The priest had one himself for he was white as a sheet, and my uncle saw that his hand was shaking.

'Give him another', said the priest, 'so that he won't see or hear anything on the way back and he won't be afraid.' And my uncle drank that one down too.

'Give him a third', said the priest. 'Well, Neil, are you afraid now?'

My uncle looked out of the window as he threw the drink into him and it was still pitch dark, with the mist rolling backwards and forwards across the countryside.

'I am still a wee bit afraid, Father', he said.

So the priest gave him another whiskey and he was afraid of nothing then and he came on home. He didn't hear anything on the bog again. But Christie was dead all right."

In many tales, the banshee is an ancestral spirit, the ghost of a person against whom a particular family has done a great wrong and who gleefully conveys a death warning to her old enemies. A tale of a banshee taking this form comes from County Kilkenny:

The Doom of the Fitzpatricks

"Just off a little side-road which leads upwards from the famous bog of Monela into the lonely Slievebloom Mountains stood at one time an almost derelict house, rearing up against the skyline close to a stand of trees. It belonged to a family named Fitzpatrick. These Fitzpatricks had a great name in the country-side for being absentee landlords, but there were many who said that they feared to live in this lonely house because of a banshee which haunted it and which followed their family. The story of this creature is one of ancient evil and great treachery.

Long ago in Ireland, around the reign of the English king, Charles I, there was a great enmity between the Fitzpatricks of Ossory and the Earls of Ormond in Kilkenny. As raids between them increased, this enmity was fanned into a bitter hatred which some say even exists to this very day. In the year that the English Charles ascended to the throne, James Butler, Earl of Ormond, completely destroyed the power of the Fitzpatricks and took

Durrow and the lands around as his own. He killed Barnaby Fitzpatrick in battle and overran Lower Ossory, putting most of the inhabitants there to the sword and demanding tributes and tithes from those that survived. The last remaining Fitzpatrick, Maurice Fitzpatrick, was forced to flee to Laois to avoid being killed himself.

There he sought sanctuary with Rory Oge O'More, one of the principal chieftains of Laois, to lick his wounds and plot revenge against the Earl of Ormond. He was regarded as an honoured guest and was treated as one of the family. Indeed, he was so completely trusted that O'More took no precautions to keep his only daughter, a very good-looking girl, away from the handsome Maurice, nor did he suspect any improper intimacy between them. His lack of suspicion was misplaced, for Maurice Fitzpatrick quickly took advantage of the young and impressionable girl and soon she was pregnant.

Secretly, she approached him and told him of her condition. Maurice, although shocked, agreed to stand by her. The lovers arranged to meet by an old well, deep in a wood near to O'More's castle from where they would elope to Scotland and be married.

At the same time, however, Rory Oge O'More began to talk about raising an army in Laois in order to aid Maurice in regaining his lands. Maurice readily encouraged this, knowing that with O'More's help he could soon drive the Earl of Ormond out of Ossory and reclaim the tithes and taxes that were his due. The only problem with the alliance was O'More's daughter. Maurice reasoned that if O'More knew that she was carrying a Fitzpatrick bastard the chieftain would withdraw his offer of help and turn the last of the Fitzpatricks out of his house. The girl had to be silenced.

O'More's daughter arrived at the appointed place by the well to find Maurice Fitzpatrick waiting for her. She ran to greet him and he swept her up into an embrace, secretly drawing a dagger as he did so. In a supreme act of treachery, Fitzpatrick plunged the dagger into the young girl's heart, killing her instantly, and dumped her body in the disused well. Then he returned to O'More's castle.

The chieftain, distraught at the disappearance of his daughter, had his serving men comb the woods and fields for days searching for her. When her body was recovered from the well, the old man's grief was absolute, but he did not link the death with Maurice Fitzpatrick. True to his treachery, Fitzpatrick kept silent as to his crime and went so far as to blame the murder on the Earl of Ormond whom, he claimed, had taken vengeance on O'More for sheltering his enemy. With the accusation, Rory Oge O'More's mind was made up. He raised an army which swept into Ossory, restoring Maurice Fitzpatrick to his former lands.

The guilty and murderous deed behind him, Fitzpatrick ruled in Ossory for many years after. The Earl of Ormond had fled to England and was now no longer a threat to him, and he married and settled down to live the life of an Irish noble. Soon he had forgotten his awful act and his lovely victim.

His business with Ormond, however, was not concluded. While in England, the Earl had used the intervening years to gain favour with the English nobility and he, himself, raised an army to return to Ireland. Many years after his expulsion, and with a substantial following of English mercenaries and Scottish gallowglasses, the Earl landed on Irish shores and marched inland towards Ossory. Many chieftains along the way made their alliances with him, for Maurice Fitzpatrick was not well liked.

By this time, Rory Oge O'More had died and his son, also called Rory, was in power in Laois. He quickly made an alliance with Ormond and turned against his father's former friend. The result was a series of battles all through Ossory and into Laois, as Maurice Fitzpatrick tried to hold onto his lands against mounting pressure.

One night, Maurice's army was camped in a wood, quite close to the long-abandoned castle of Rory Oge O'More. It had been a long time since Maurice had been there and he did not recognise the spot. His men were being harried by Ormond's forces and were being pushed back to the borders of Laois where they were regrouping for a final battle. As Maurice sat with his captains by a roaring open fire, planning the strategy for the fight, he was seized with a terrible thirst.

'Bring me some water', he asked his servant. The servant disappeared and returned several minutes later bearing a goblet. Maurice drank long and deep, then suddenly spat out the fluid in his mouth.

'What is this?' he shouted. 'Why have you brought me a goblet of blood to drink?'

The servant looked uncomprehendingly into the container.

'It is water, sir', he answered. 'I brought it myself from an old well deep in these woodlands.'

Then Maurice looked around him and, recognising where he was, remembered his dreadful act of years before. Through the hanging branches of the surrounding trees, he saw a blood-stained figure, in flowing robes, looking directly at him. In that instant, he saw O'More's daughter whom he had murdered. The figure opened its mouth and gave a high, wailing shriek as it pointed towards the terrified chieftain. The soldiers around the fire crossed themselves quickly for, although they saw nothing, they recognised the cry of the banshee.

As the accusing figure stretched forth her arms towards him, Maurice Fitzpatrick fell to his knees and shouted, 'Pardon! Oh pardon your murderer!'

The soldiers around him muttered and edged away, for they thought that their leader was taking leave of his senses. The apparition gave another harsh scream and vanished like a veil of mist. Her screams, however, continued to echo through that ancient woodland, fading away as the first fingers of the rising sun touched the horizon. Hardly had the final scream died away than there came a shout from the sentinel on the edge of the camp. A large force of both O'Mores and Butlers were attacking!

Despite his terror, Maurice Fitzpatrick drew his sword and joined in the fray. The battle was a long and bloody one but in the end the Earl of Ormond's forces were triumphant and Maurice and several of his lieutenants lay dead. The banshee's warning had come to pass.

After this, the cry of the banshee followed the Fitzpatricks, and in time it became so notorious that the spring where the murder had occurred became known as the 'Banshee's Well'. No matter when or where a Fitzpatrick died, in battle or in bed, at home or abroad, the event was signalled by a wailing in the woods which was frequently heard by travellers in that area.

In the course of time, the Fitzpatricks themselves were expelled from Ossory and were forced to settle in Laois, in the district of the O'Mores, where Maurice's descendants built a mansion. There they lived, off and on, for some years. Throughout much of the eighteenth century, the banshee remained silent and the story of her vengeful cry became little more than a legend amongst the Fitzpatrick family.

However, around the end of the nineteenth century, one of the

Fitzpatrick daughters fell ill. The doctors diagnosed it as little more than a passing fever and confined the girl to bed. That evening, her father was out walking around the back of the house when he saw, in the stand of trees which marked the outer reaches of an old woodland, a woman standing, watching the house. She appeared to be wearing some sort of white garment, seemingly covered in blood. Thinking it to be some trespasser, he walked towards her to ask her what she wanted but she only pointed in the direction of the house and issued a blood-curdling shriek. Even as he watched her, she faded away and was gone. Terrified, he ran back to the house where he found his daughter in a deep sleep.

Throughout the following days, the child seemed to recover a little, although she remained in bed. Three days later the girl was sitting up in bed as night was drawing on when, suddenly, she pointed to the window opposite her bed.

'Who is that beautiful lady covered in blood?' she asked.

A nurse who was dozing by the fire wakened with a start, just in time to see the pale face of a woman, bloodily smeared, drawing back from the window. From somewhere outside came the thin, wailing sound of the banshee. Crossing herself against evil, the nurse turned back to the young girl who had fallen in a swoon, a swoon from which she did not recover. She died the following day.

After that, the grieving parents forsook the house and went to live in England. Soon even the remaining servants left and the house stood alone and untended near the lone stand of trees by the road which leads to the uninhabited mountains.''

The Devil

In rural Ireland, the barrier between life and death was often fragile. Men working the land or fishing the seas might easily meet with an unexpected and fatal accident. Disease also frequently attacked isolated communities with tragic results. Such misfortunes served to remind the people of their own mortality and reinforced the idea of the imminence of evil in their daily lives.

The Church taught that the souls of those that had died suddenly and without benefit of priest or clergy would automatically be claimed by the devil unless they had led an exceptionally good life. Consequently Satan was very close. He loitered in isolated and dangerous areas – along the seashore, close to deep bogs, at the tops of steep hills or cliffs – anxious to pull the spirits of the unfortunate down to everlasting torment.

When at his dark tasks, he took on a variety of forms in order to disguise his true identity. An old prayer from County Derry states that he lurks, "in the mist on the mountain, in the blaze of a winter's fire, in the whin bush or in the dark hollow; from his coming and going about the world, oh Lord, protect us."

Sometimes he appeared as nothing more substantial than a shadow, flitting through the late evening sunshine. Sometimes he took a more tangible form, such as that of an animal, usually a cat or dog. Indeed, as late as 1952, the devil in canine form is said to have appeared to a young girl in County Wicklow.

The Tale of Margo Ryan

"I knew Margo Ryan well enough. She was a quiet and very pleasant girl who came from a good family that lived out near Redcross. Decent farming people they were.

Now, this evening she was carrying home a large can of buttermilk from a neighbouring farm. She was travelling between the lights which is always a very bad time on the roads. If you are to see things which are not of this mortal world, then you will usually see them between the lights, that's a well known fact. It was all very quiet as she went – a grand evening at the end of summer – and there wasn't another living thing to be seen on that country road.

She quickened her step so as to be home before it turned completely dark when, all of a sudden, she heard a soft 'pad pad' sound behind her. It was the sound of some animal following her on the road and, although she was afraid to turn round and see it, it soon drew level with her. It was a big, black dog, about the size of a young calf, walking along the road and keeping step with her. She spoke to it but the dog never turned; it just kept on walking alongside her. She didn't know whose animal it was – she didn't recognise it as belonging to any of her neighbours – and it frightened her a wee bit, for she thought that it might be a strange, vicious dog which might turn on her and attack her.

Well, after a time, Margo's courage rallied a little and she thought that the dog mightn't touch her after all, for it seemed quiet and friendly enough. So she reached out a hand to pat its back. Lord save us, didn't her hand go right through it as if it had been no more than smoke! And she could still see the animal plainly enough. For a minute, she thought that she had been mistaken and that the evening light had tricked her so she reached out to stroke its back again but she felt nothing, only the empty air. Still the dog was beside her, walking along the road as calmly as you like, matching her step for step, and still she could hear the sound of its passing steps clearly. Margo realised that the animal was so much taller than she was that it would be impossible for her to reach up and get a hold of it.

Then, and only then, the hound turned its head to look at her and she saw that it had long and sharp teeth, by far the biggest she had ever seen, and that its chin was all white and grizzled, and slavering with slabbers. And the very fires of hell were burning behind its red eyes. Margo knew then that this was no ordinary dog but something supernatural, maybe even the devil himself, come from the world below to take her away with him. She was so frightened that she stopped where she was and cried out, calling on the name of Our Saviour and His Mother and all the holy angels and saints.

The dog walked a little bit ahead of her and then turned round. With the fire still blazing in its eyes, it gave a low growl, turned its head to the left and vanished like the mist in the morning. There was no other way to describe it – it just disappeared!

Let there be no doubt about it. It didn't run off or turn off into a field, for one minute it was there in front of her and the next it was gone. It had been standing in the very centre of the road so it couldn't have jumped off into the hedge. Besides, there was no gap through which it could have gone, only a bank at the side of the road which it would have had to climb. It was a ghostly thing all right, something sent from the very pits of hell to follow the wee girl on the quiet road.

They say that the devil is always after the souls of the good and innocent ones. Only Margo was such a good girl and always went to mass, it would have had her, true enough!"

Sometimes the devil also prowled the countryside in feline form and strange cats were often looked on with suspicion. At times of great communal distress he might also appear in human form as a stranger, often that of a handsome or well-dressed man.

The Blacksmith and the Devil

"There was a blacksmith who used to have a forge just beyond Raphoe in Donegal and his name was Yellow Billy. They say that there was no-one could touch him at the smithying for he was the best blacksmith in the whole of Donegal and in six other counties as well. The nobility came from all over, bringing their horses to him to be shod, so great was his name in the country. Now, the events about which I am going to tell you happened at a particular time when there was great disease and misfortune throughout Donegal.

It was late one night, just at the very edge of dark, and Yellow Billy was finishing up some work that he had been doing, intending to shut up for the night. He was smoking on a pipe of tobacco and was putting some tools away when he heard the sound of a horse in his yard. Looking out, he saw that a stranger had ridden in. Although it was near dark, he could see that the man had a long, grand riding-coat on him and a cocked hat with a yellow plume in it and that he was mounted on a fine, dusky horse that almost merged with the gloom outside.

Yellow Billy stifled a curse for he had planned to close up and go home to sit by the fire. His wife had a good meal cooking for him and he hoped to finish the day by a roaring blaze with a glass of porter. The last thing that he needed was someone wanting his horse to be shod. But business was business, so he went out to see what the man wanted.

The stranger looked down at him from under the cocked hat and although Yellow Billy could make out his eyes, which sparkled like stars, he couldn't make out the other's face at all, for most of it was hidden by the evening shadow.

'I have ridden hard and long', said the man without any sort of introduction, 'and I still have a long way to go. My horse needs shod and I am told that you are the best blacksmith in these parts.' Yellow Billy bowed low at the compliment from such a fine gentleman.

'Indeed, I would be proud to shoe your honour's horse', said he, 'but the hour is getting late and my dinner is warming on the hearth-stone. Perhaps, if your honour were to come back first thing in the morning, I could take a look at his horse then.'

The other gave a loud and impatient sigh.

'My business in this district is most urgent', he replied, 'and I must be gone before morning. My horse needs only the one shoe fitted. If you were to attend to it now, I would make it well worth your while.' And, digging deep into the pocket of his grand coat, he produced a gold sovereign which seemed to shine brightly in the failing light. Yellow Billy's eyes widened for this was the most that he had ever been offered for putting on the one shoe. Still, he was anxious to be home and at his supper.

'But the fire in my forge has burned down, your honour, and it will take a while to get it going again', he protested.

The stranger waved that excuse away.

'I think', said he, 'that if you look into your smithy, you will see the forge as hot as ever.' And when Yellow Billy looked into the smithy sure enough, the forge was burning brighter than ever. It filled the entire smithy with a dull and ruddy glow and was as if he had just left working at it. There was little more that he could say.

'If your honour will bring the horse forward, I will shoe him right away.' The stranger nodded and started to dismount.

'One moment', he said when he had reached the ground. 'I will need to see the nails that you intend to use.'

His request puzzled Yellow Billy for, as long as he had been a blacksmith, no-one had asked him anything about the nails he used for shoeing horses. He went into the smithy and brought out a handful of iron nails.

'They are just ordinary iron nails', he answered, 'the same as I would use for shoeing any other horse.'

But the stranger shook his head, his star-like eyes shining.

'They will not do.'

He dug once more into the pocket of his coat and brought out several other nails, made of a type of metal such as Yellow Billy had never seen before.

'My horse is a very special animal and you will have to use these nails. I think you'll find that they do just as well as iron ones.'

Yellow Billy took the nails in his hand and they felt heavier than those that he was used to.

'Very well', he told the stranger, 'I'll use your nails. Now bring the horse forward into the smithy.'

The stranger led the dusky horse forward and Yellow Billy saw that the man walked with a strange, halting step as though he had a club-foot.

Whilst the blacksmith was shoeing the horse, the stranger sat in the doorway of the smithy smoking a long pipe which he had lit from the forge, and looked out into the night. He didn't speak to Yellow Billy, nor the blacksmith to him.

At last the job was finished. The stranger rose and hobbled over to the animal.

'It is a task well done, blacksmith', says he and, taking the gold coin from his pocket, he laid it on the very edge of the anvil.

'Now, if you will help me into the saddle, I'll trouble you no further.'

And, as the dusky horse stood obediently, the blacksmith gave the stranger a lift up onto its back.

As he did so, however, a sudden gust of wind swirled through the door and caught the end of the stranger's long riding-coat, blowing it up a little ways. As it did so, Yellow Billy caught a glimpse of the stranger's foot beneath the coat and he saw that it wasn't a human foot at all. It was the cleft foot of an animal, like that of a goat or cow. Then he knew that the stranger was the devil, who had been causing so much misfortune in the countryside, and that he had shod his horse. That was why he could not use the iron nails, for the fiends of hell fear holy iron more than any other metal except silver.

Crossing himself, he turned quickly in time to see the gold coin on the edge of the anvil vanish in a puff of smoke, leaving a dark mark where it had lain on the metal. The stranger, too, vanished clean away, as if he had never been there at all. One moment he was in front of the startled blacksmith and the next he had faded away like the mist before the sun. But Yellow Billy heard the sound of the horse's hooves, galloping into the twilight, though he could see nothing.

That was a true story for my grandmother, who was a Donegal woman, often talked about the man who shoed the devil's horse and she said that she had seen the anvil with the black mark still on it where the devil's money had lain."

*Despite such frightening encounters, some tales reveal the devil
to be quite an agreeable character and one who might be quite
readily made a fool of. An old and humorous story concerning
the parish of Loughguile, in the East Antrim hills, serves as an
example. It also concerns a gold coin and explains how the
largest expanse of water in the area – Lough Guile (the Lake of
Weeping) – got its name.*

The Lake of Weeping

"There was a priest one time on Loughguile called Father
Mullan. He was very fond of a drink and nothing pleased him
more than to sit up by the lough with a bottle and a fishing-line
to see what he could catch. They said that he drank among the
fairies up there as well, but I'm not sure as to the truth of that.
No decent Christian person, let alone a priest, would consort
with the Gentry.

Anyhow, one warm summer's day he was out on his rambles
when he came upon the devil sitting on a big rock, taking his ease
in the sun. The oul' boy was half-dozing, puffing on a Scotch
pipe (an old long-stemmed pipe) and was resting after a hard day
at tempting people.

Now, I heard that all this happened on the top of Groog
Mountain, whilst some say that it was over by the old Giant's
Bed in Tobernagrollagh, but nobody is really sure. What I do
know is that Father Mullan wanted the devil out of his parish but
that he wasn't sure how to go about it. He decided to be very
cunning: he would be very civil to him in order to find out
whatever weaknesses he might have and see how he could use
them against him.

He sat down opposite the devil and the oul' boy woke up with a start. Seeing the priest, he began to splutter, expecting all manner of crucifixes and rosaries to be waved in his face, but Father Mullan told him to sit quiet and take his ease for he only wanted a rest, and they could both enjoy the day like two civilised creatures.

'How are things with you?' asked the priest.

'A bit slow', admitted the devil, taking a draw on the pipe. 'There are far too many good thoughts and prayers in this parish for my liking. You're doing a good job here. My compliments to you. At this rate, hell will be missing a few souls this year all right.'

The priest nodded and looked out over the countryside.

'Is hell really as bad as they say?' he asked. 'I only know what I hear about it, of course.'

The devil shrugged.

'It's no worse than anyplace else', he said. 'Of course, it's not fire and brimstone all the time. We have some grand times there too. There's ceili-ing, card-playing and dancing for as long as you like and there's always plenty of poteen to be had. Aye, the crack there's very good from time to time.'

The priest nodded again.

'And what about heaven?' he asked. 'Is it really the paradise that they say it is?'

The devil took another draw on his pipe.

'I haven't been there for a long time', he answered at last. 'Not since I was cast out. It's probably all changed now. But my recollection of it was that it was an awfully dreary place. No ceilis or wagering, and definitely no poteen. Everybody just sat around looking beatific and sang hymns all day. Where's the fun in that? If my memory is right, it wasn't a place that you'd even like to go to for a bit of a night, let alone for all eternity.'

Father Mullan nodded sagely.

'True enough', he answered. 'If all those that think they're going to heaven actually get there, it must be a sour, dry place indeed.'

'It strikes me that you're a man who likes a bit of crack yourself', said the devil slyly, always anxious to make up his quota of lost souls from the parish. 'You'd like hell all right. Maybe I could put you down for ...'

But the priest waved away that suggestion.

So the conversation went on after this fashion for some time and the priest found that the devil was a right civil being, for the oul' boy liked his drink just as much as he himself did.

Now, it so happened that Father Mullan had a bottle of poteen on him and he offered it to the devil. Soon they were talking and laughing together as if they'd known each other for years.

'Is it true that you can do anything?' asked the priest, very innocent.

'I can, to be sure', hiccupped the devil, who was beginning to feel the effects of the strong drink.

'And can you take any shape at all?' went on Father Mullan.

'I can rightly', answered the devil. 'Any shape you care to name.'

And so saying, he took the form of a goat, of a great black crow, of a monstrous hound, of a bull with the head of a child, of a chair made out of bones and of a woman with a beard.

The priest, however, was not impressed.

'That's all very well', he said, 'but I bet you couldn't take the shape of something like ... oh ... a gold sovereign?'

'Nothing easier', said the devil, who was by this time rightly intoxicated, and he turned himself into a gold coin.

'Now I have you!' shouted Father Mullan and he immediately

snapped up the sovereign and put it into a purse which he sealed by anointing it with holy water. Try as he might, the devil couldn't get out of the purse.

'I should have known better than to trust a priest!' he shouted angrily.

'So you should', replied Father Mullan. And so saying, he went over to the edge of the water at Loughguile and threw the purse into the water.

'There you'll stay until the Day of Judgement and you'll never bother my parish again.'

And that's the way of it up until the present day. They say that the devil is still under the water up at Loughguile, still trying to get out. That's why they call the place Lough Guile (the "lake of weeping" in the old Irish). If you happen to be passing by the lake on a moonlit night, you'll hear him calling out and crying and it's best to walk on quickly. If you were to find the purse and take out the gold coin, sure wouldn't the devil be free in Loughguile parish again."